Accept No
Limitations

Accept No Limitations

A Black Woman Encounters Corporate America

MARJORIE L. KIMBROUGH

ABINGDON PRESS
Nashville

ACCEPT NO LIMITATIONS

Copyright © 1991 by Abingdon Press

Second Printing 1991

This book is printed on acid-free paper.

Library of Congress Cataloging-in-Publication Data

Kimbrough, Marjorie L., 1937–
  Accept no limitations: a black woman encounters corporate America
/Marjorie L. Kimbrough.
    p. cm.
  ISBN 0-687-00694-5 (alk. paper)
  1. Kimbrough, Marjorie L., 1937– . 2. Afro-American women-
-Biography. 3. Afro-American mathematicians—Biography. 4. Afro-
American women—Employment. 5. Discrimination in employment—
United States. I. Title.
HD6057.5.U5K56   1991
[B]   90-47400
                                                                       CIP

MANUFACTURED IN THE UNITED STATES OF AMERICA

To my husband, who encouraged and supported the writing of this book;
To my mother, who always told me I was better; and
To all my friends and relatives, who really believe I am.

FOREWORD

I have constantly argued that authentic integration is not the systematic movement of all things Black to all things white, but the emphatic movement of all things wrong to all things right! Once we thought that all Afro-Americans had to do to achieve full citizenship was to move into the American mainstream. The more we attempt, however, the more we discover that the mainstream is morally and ethically polluted.

Marge Kimbrough's experience, which she describes in simple but graphic fashion, is not only a testimony to her gifts, self-confidence, and tenacity, but also a clear affirmation of the "pollution" of the mainstream. The corporate community has an invisible wall beyond which Blacks cannot pass as well as an invincible ceiling above which we shall not rise!

A Black woman looks squarely in the face of a double-barreled missile of racism and sexism (white women face sexism).

The book is written in down-to-earth language and style and may be read with rhythmic flow. Armed with faith, unusual talent, and an abundance of self-confidence, the author is able to deal with the "pollution" with intelligence and emotional and spiritual maturity.

It is important that young Blacks who seek careers and

fulfillment in the corporate jungle have a firm base in spirituality and self-esteem. All of our institutions today—especially the Church and home—must prepare our young people for the turbulence by having their seat-belts of self-understanding, self-esteem, and spiritual grounding firmly fastened.

This is a valuable book for corporate executives as well. The corporation that fails to maximize opportunities for talented employees who are Black, Brown, male or female—is also the loser, and so is the nation.

I hear this book crying in the wilderness for Afro-Americans to approach the future with a sense of mission—to purify the mainstream—not just for integration but for regeneration; not just for adjustment, but for justice.

For this role to which we have been called, we must put on the whole armor of God and engage in the struggle for a revival of values with ethical and moral bases in the marketplace.

This book ought to be, among other places, in college libraries, *and* corporate board rooms! Amen!

The Reverend Joseph E. Lowery
Senior Minister, Cascade United Methodist Church
President, Southern Christian Leadership Conference
Atlanta

CONTENTS

1. *To Be the Best*.. 13

2. *Los Angeles*... 15

3. *Atlanta*.. 27

4. *Marriage + School + Work*............................37

5. *Chicago*..45

6. *Babies*.. 55

7. *Teaching Graduate School*............................ 65

8. *Returning to the Corporate South*.................73

9. *Upward Mobility*..79

10. *Corruption Abounds*....................................... 93

11. *Changes in Management*........................... 105

12. *Becoming the Trainer*................................. 117

13. *Deciding on a New Life*.............................. 131

    Epilogue.. 139

Accept No
Limitations

1

To Be the Best

Although I did not realize it at the time, my mother started preparing me for my encounter with corporate America when I began nursery school. I noticed that most of the other children were lighter than I was, and all of the teachers were. My mother stressed being good, better, best. She said, "You must be the best one, the smartest, because 'they' will not expect it of you." As I grew older I realized that white people believe that black people are inferior; they do not, to quote former Los Angeles Dodgers' executive Al Campanis, have the 'necessities' to lead or manage.[1] I have discovered through my corporate American encounter that most white people agree with Mr. Campanis and sincerely believe that black people are not equipped intellectually to think, work, study, or exist in the world alone—that is, without the help of white people.

My mother warned me that white people would expect me to be inferior, even stupid, but I was determined to fool them. I decided, with Mama's encouragement, to be better, to be the best; and I was. I was valedictorian of my graduating class at

---

1. Al Campanis made these remarks during a nationally televised interview with ABC correspondent Ted Koppel at the beginning of the 1987 baseball season. In the wake of furor following the broadcast, Mr. Campanis was fired by the Dodgers.

Berkeley High in Berkeley, California; it was the first time that a black student had led all the others.

This legacy followed me to the University of California at Berkeley, where again it was necessary to perform at the level of the best. Because I wanted to do this so badly, I chose mathematics as my field of major study. I knew that while one's efforts in many subjects are evaluated subjectively (at the whim of some white instructor's feeling or judgment), mathematics is evaluated objectively. A mathematically right or wrong answer leaves no room for whim. When it came to mathematics, I did not have to concern myself either with how the instructor felt about my being a black student or with how he felt about himself in evaluating a black student, for my answers were either correct or they were not.

In 1959 I was graduated Phi Beta Kappa and accepted a position as a mathematical analyst at Lockheed Aircraft Corporation in Burbank, California. This was the first of several positions that would place me in a previously all-white department or all-white company. But I was prepared because I was accustomed to being the only black face in the crowd. Or so I thought.

2

Los Angeles

For as long as I could remember, Berkeley had been my home. It was known as the bedroom community to San Francisco and Oakland, having a population of about one hundred thousand in 1959. Its claim to fame was the University from which I had just been graduated. During my tenure, the University had not yet developed its radical reputation, for invasion by the flower children and hippies occurred later, during the 1960s. I was moving away from my quiet home in Berkeley to a rented apartment in Los Angeles with a population of approximately two million. The newness of my physical relocation was enough to cause considerable apprehension as I began my career in corporate America. However, in addition to my personal adjustment, I had to deal with the uneasiness my Lockheed co-workers experienced because of my presence. I was the first black mathematical analyst ever hired, but I believed that if I proved myself to be competent, I would be accepted.

I was wrong. No matter how competent I was, there were still conversations in which I was not included; there were still restaurants, yes, even in liberal Southern California, in which I was not welcome; and there were still suspicions that I had been hired to satisfy federal contract demands. Any of these events individually, and certainly any combination of them, could have contributed to a feeling of insecurity if it were not for the fact that I had been trained—even indoctrinated—with a sense of being better than the others, even being the best. So I ignored the looks, glances, and snickers, and I began to learn my job and establish relationships in spite of them all.

On a one-to-one basis, there were individuals who were very accepting, liberal, and loving; but many others simply *knew* that a black female just did not belong in a technical job, especially one almost exclusively held by white males. The Women's Liberation Movement had not begun in 1959, so there were many males who did not believe that any woman, black or white, belonged in a technical job. In fact, many of my male co-workers felt that most women belonged either at home or working in teaching or clerical positions.

During that first year in the mathematical analysis department, I aligned and identified with the white women who were happy to see other working women joining the technical ranks. Some of those friendships lasted throughout my twenty-eight-year venture in corporate America. They are truly sisters under the skin. The relationships with the white men were quite different. Those who had supervisory status accepted me as one who needed to be protected and directed. They were somewhat awed by this high level of attainment for a black woman, and they decided to accept the challenge of managing me. They sincerely believed that I had no notion of further advancement, for surely I could not possibly handle a position like theirs.

Those white men who, regrettably, were my peers resented the fact that a black woman could have the same job and title as they did. That surely cheapened or lessened the position. I remembered learning long ago that the only way some people can feel superior is by diligently seeking to keep others inferior, and job status is definitely one way of accomplishing that.

One white male peer from Oklahoma decided to harass me.

My desk was next to his, and this seating arrangement was more than he could bear. I was determined not to complain, but my white sisters complained for me. They said that they would not take the slurs and criticism he dispensed, and neither should I. I was moved; the Oklahoman was ostracized and eventually fired. This action seemed to serve as a warning that I should be treated with kindness, or at least with indifference.

This incident showed that my white co-workers were willing to rally to support me. They generally felt that this lone black woman was different from all of those other black people, and she should be defended and protected. They also wanted me to believe that the Oklahoman was an isolated Southerner who harbored prejudices that were foreign to the rest of them. I have often wondered what would have happened if there had been several black co-workers. I have noticed that while one black is accepted, several are rejected because they, as a group, are considered to be threatening.

My new desk neighbor, also a white male, decided to try to discover the real me and asked to visit me at my apartment. Although I liked him, I was not interested in establishing an after-work relationship with him. Once we had the understanding that a visit would just be a visit and that neither of us was interested in anything more intimate, I invited him to my apartment. He found out what I had known all along—that black women are just like all women. They have dreams, aspirations, loves, and woes. We agreed that under different circumstances we might have established a closer relationship, but 1959 was not in my estimation the time for interracial involvement—not even in California.

However, I observed that for many black men, it *was* the time. Several black professional men were involved in interracial relationships. I suppose this involvement stemmed from the black man/white woman relationships that were forbidden during slavery. Whereas black women were forced into relationships with white men, black men were denied all alliances with white women. The advent of freedom and professionalism encouraged the black male to seek what had previously been denied him. Thus, I did observe black males with white females, and I resented it. Several interracial couples lived in the apartment complex where I lived, and it was very apparent that the couple had become black. The white woman had left her predominantly white neighborhood for the black or mixed one. The white woman could become black, but the black woman in a similar situation could never become white. Her partner would also have to become black, for there was no chance of her being accepted in his white community. Although there were several white women with black men in the apartment complex, there was only one black woman living with a white man. The only vandalism that I can remember occurring during the years I lived there was the setting of this man's car on fire. The white woman had been accepted; the white man had not.

My relationship with white men was strictly professional, but my relationship with white women was personal. Being the only black employee in the department, some close personal friendships were bound to develop, and I shared many non-business hours with one woman in particular. This black-white friendship was not new to me, as many of my close personal friends both at Berkeley High and at the University of California were white. There was, however, one thing new about this friendship; it was the first time that I had been close to a white female who was about the same age and married. This new circumstance caused a problem that I had not expected.

I spent a good deal of time with my friend and her husband. On one occasion the husband and I were alone. As we discussed the personal concerns I had as a black woman in an all-white work environment, he sought to comfort me. I took this act of comfort for a sexual advance. I responded by telling him that I was not that kind of woman, and I reprimanded him because his wife and I were best friends. He told his wife what had happened, and she explained what he had intended and apologized. I still wonder why his act of comfort came in the absence of his wife.

This episode introduced another element of interracial involvement. I had been warned not to spend too much time, as a single woman, around married couples, but I had thought that this warning did not apply to white couples. It could not possibly apply to white couples because the warning was issued to avoid a single woman's coming between a husband and wife. I had no intention of trying to come between my friend and her husband; yet I interpreted his actions as actually causing me to do just that. Again, I was learning that men are men and women are women no matter what the color.

Lockheed, then, served not only as an introduction to corporate America, but also as an introduction to interracial male-female relationships. Although I attended predominantly white institutions of learning, I had never become socially involved, on a personal level, with white men. I suppose my youth and sexual inexperience accounted for this, though it is still true more than thirty years later that blacks who attend predominantly white schools form their own racially segregated social groups. Fraternities and sororities are, and will continue to be, segregated. In addition, I knew that my parents would have frowned upon my dating or socializing with white males.

The novelty of my being the first black in Lockheed's mathematical analysis department grew as pictures were taken of me for use with reports to the federal government. Because Lockheed was a federal contractor, it was necessary to prove that minorities were being hired and treated without discrimination on the job. So the pictures were used to show that I had the same sort of desk, chair, and telephone as everyone else; that I was sitting next to other employees (no one mentioned the fellow from Oklahoma); and that I was not being denied any of the rights entitled to other employees. All of this attention served to make my co-workers feel that I was different (from other blacks)—special—for surely the federal government would not be interested in just any black. Again, their acceptance of me as the only black in the group had been justified, for indeed I was exceptional. The cameras had verified it.

This was not the only time the cameras passed by the security guards to take my picture, for during my tenure with Lockheed my picture appeared in the "Speaking of People" section of *Ebony* Magazine. Although most of my co-workers were not familiar with this black publication, the fact that I had been selected to appear in it served to further confirm their feeling that I was special. After my picture, age, position, and salary were published, I began to receive fan mail at the office. There were congratulatory remarks, proposals of marriage, suggestions of sexual affairs, and requests for regular correspondence. I had not expected such a response to the magazine appearance.

Upon reflection, I am sure that this celebrity status was resented by my peers, for the only real difference between them and me was the color of my skin. I was performing the same job, but because I was the first black to do so, I was recognized in a way that they were not. I am sure that many of them realized that I was not being treated equally, but differently—perhaps even better.

This special recognition did not, however, extend to special job recognition. I received the same cost of living increases that everyone else did, and I received very average merit raises and promotions. I was promoted to mathematical engineer, the highest position to which one could be promoted without serving as a supervisor of others. I left Lockheed to go to graduate school before it would have been necessary to promote me to group engineer. I wonder what excuse would have been given for my not getting the promotion. I did observe that very few women held the position of group engineer, and, of course, there were no blacks. About the time that my friend would have been considered for group engineer, she went on maternity leave.

Lockheed provided me with a real introduction to the corporate world. There were lewd office comments, dirty jokes, illicit affairs, and all of the real-world components to which I had not been exposed either at home or in college. At first the white men were somewhat embarrassed to tell dirty jokes in front of me, but as they became more familiar with me as a "normal" person, they relaxed and began to show me the same disrespect they showed the white women. I am sure that this was because they had decided that I was more like white women than black women. After all, I had gotten special celebrity treatment.

There also were real acts of concern for me as I had major surgery during my tenure with Lockheed. While I lived, socialized, received medical care, and worshiped in a predominantly black environment, I worked in a predominantly white one. The black doctor who provided my medical care necessarily practiced in a black hospital, and my white co-workers had never been to the inner-city neighborhood near the University of Southern California campus in which I was hospitalized. I lived in Los Angeles, but Lockheed was in Burbank, and my co-workers lived in the white Los Angeles suburbs. Most of my co-workers sent get well cards or inquired about me through my pastor. I lived alone, but everyone knew that I was very active in my church and felt that my pastor could answer their questions about my condition. Only one co-worker, an elderly white woman, dared to come to visit me, after dark, in the hospital. I have never forgotten her visit.

I convalesced at home for several weeks, and as soon as I was well enough to go out to dinner, my group engineer invited me to a Beverly Hills restaurant. He felt uneasy about the invitation and immediately explained that his wife and one of his children, who was celebrating a birthday, would accompany us. The black-white/male-female issue continued to enter into every relationship—even those in which a boss was trying to be kind to an employee recovering from major surgery. Although I felt that my boss had no ulterior motives in extending the dinner invitation, I was glad that his wife and daughter would be joining us. I would have been very uncomfortable dining alone with a man who was married, white, and my supervisor. During the dinner, we did not encounter the stares that usually accompanied my attending eating establishments alone in the company of white men. I eventually learned to ignore those stares, for they were to be with me throughout my career.

While at Lockheed, I did attempt to establish some social connections by joining the company choir. I had been accustomed to extra-curricular activities during my college career, and I had discovered that music is one of the avenues used to bridge racial barriers. However, there were very few blacks participating in the choir. Rehearsals were scheduled during normal working hours, but performances were at company meetings and other events that involved a long commute for blacks who did not live in the communities with white choir members. Also, hourly workers found it more difficult to be excused from their jobs for rehearsals than salaried workers, and most black workers were hourly. I never felt particularly comfortable in the Lockheed choir, and my participation in it was limited. I am sure that the source of my discomfort lay in the fact that no one else from my department was in the choir. Therefore I was not special to any of the white participants. The blacks with whom they worked were very ordinary. There had been no *Ebony* pictures or federal cameras; I was just one among many. Although I made an effort, I was never made to feel welcome. I guess there were too many other more important barriers to overcome—such as learning the job, feeling racially accepted in the primary work group, and living alone—to bother with this social one.

After almost five years at Lockheed, I began to do some personal reassessment. I felt that I could rather comfortably continue to work as a mathematical engineer for several years if governmental contracts continued and there were no drastic layoffs. But I knew that I wanted more than Lockheed could offer. I did not see myself being promoted to a project leader or group engineer, for there were no blacks in those positions; and during the four and one half years that I had been there, no other blacks had even been hired in my department. I also realized that I spent most of my waking hours at work, and my prospects for meeting eligible bachelors were limited. I had been raised in a time when having a husband and a family were signs of successful womanhood. I really wanted it all, but the marriage and the family were definitely a priority. I felt that I would always have my career, as the skills I had developed in the data processing industry would be in demand anywhere I went. But there were probably some areas where my prospects of finding a husband might be better.

I considered what I really liked about the job and what I disliked. I enjoyed the challenge of solving technical problems, working with people, and programming the computer, but I did not enjoy sitting behind a metal desk all day. I considered my options and decided to go to graduate school in the South. I had never lived in the South (except as a very young child), and I believed that attending a predominantly black school would provide me with possible marriage prospects.

I had always wanted to obtain a degree in Christian education, for I felt that children must have a distorted idea of God because they are taught by professionals every day in public school, but when they attend Sunday school they are taught by amateurs (usually poor ones at that). I knew that there was a more professional way to teach Sunday school and to impart to children the importance of God and his teachings.

So, with the prospect of improving my marriage potential, with the opportunity of attending a black school and being taught by black instructors (my exposure to black teachers had been extremely limited in California), and with the challenge of living and working in the South, I submitted my resignation. The reaction to my resignation was mostly negative. My co-workers wondered where they had gone wrong. How could I possibly want to leave the safe, protective environment that they offered for the racial bigotry of the South?

Again and again they expressed feelings that I suspected they had held all along: "Margie, don't go down there. *They* won't know who you are. *They* will treat you like all of *those* people." (*They* referred to the Southern whites, and *those* referred to the Southern blacks.) The particular brand of racism practiced in California in the 1960s was perceived as being more honorable than the brand practiced in the South. After all, there were no sit-ins or other demonstrations taking place in California; most of the schools were as integrated as the neighborhoods; and Martin Luther King was leading the boycott in Montgomery, not Los Angeles. My white co-workers felt pretty comfortable about themselves and very protective of me. I was special, and once I got to the South with all of those other blacks, the whites would not know me from all the others.

I packed my belongings. I was encouraged to get my master's degree in California or at least in the North, but I wanted to go South. I had chosen the Interdenominational Theological Center, a part of the Atlanta University Center. The Master of Religious Education degree entailed a two-year course of study, and Atlanta had long been recognized not only as a center of black higher education, but also as an oasis in the South. I promised to return after I obtained my degree, and my supervisor said that there would be a job for me. No one really expected me to return, but I was hoping to come back with both an MRE and an MRS degree.

I left Lockheed, having been introduced to Corporate America. I had been accepted on an individual basis, but I had not seen any real acceptance of others in my race. I received the same raises and promotions that the other women received, but these did not compare with what the men were receiving. No women were promoted to supervisory positions during my four and one-half-year tenure, and no other blacks were hired. I learned that there are many sexual overtones to office conversation and that male-female relationships certainly cross racial lines. I also rediscovered the kinship that exists among women of all races, for they suffer the same injustices. I learned a lot, but there was so much more yet to learn. My corporate encounter would reveal atrocious disparities as I moved to the South.

3

Atlanta

*E*nrolling in graduate school was easy; finding a part-time job was not. Older Atlantans who were familiar with Southern atrocities referred me to the Atlanta Urban League. I was told that it would be difficult for me to find a position similar to the one I had held at Lockheed in California. I was told that black men and women were just not employed as mathematical engineers. In addition, my being a black female who wanted to work part-time further complicated things. Part-time professional positions were not even available for white females. But I was determined, and I responded to an advertisement placed by Burroughs Corporation for a programmer who knew the FORTRAN programming language (a scientific programming language whose name is derived from Formula Translation).

When I appeared in the Atlanta district office with my résumé in hand, people stopped and stared. The receptionist's mouth flew open when I told her why I was there. Although my Lockheed co-workers had also stared, they were not so bold about it, for I had been hired during a campus interview and the recruiter had told everyone that I was black. These Burroughs workers had not been forewarned. The job to which I responded involved translating some FORTRAN programs into the Burroughs assembler code, and it could be handled on a part-time basis. The problem was that I did not know the Burroughs assembler language. However, I did know FOR-TRAN, and I was convinced that learning any assembler code had to be within the realm of possibility for me. After all, my mother had taught me that I was the smartest one in the class, and lack of self-confidence was foreign to me.

The manager who interviewed me explained that I would be the first black professional hired by Burroughs in the South. (The Atlanta district office in which I would be working did have a black man in the mail/supply room, but no other black employees.) I was also told that there was only one restaurant in the vicinity to which I could go for service and be seated and treated like other paying customers. (That restaurant was the Davis Brothers Cafeteria on West Peachtree Street.) I could go to one other lunch counter and place a carry-out order at the window, but I could not sit at that counter. This was 1963 in Atlanta, Georgia, and I could not believe what I was hearing. How could it possibly be that I was not good enough to sit down in any restaurant I wanted to and be served like anyone else? This certainly was not in keeping with what Mama had told me. Who in their right mind could not want me to eat in their restaurant? But then I remembered that in California there had been a couple of restaurants in which I would not have been welcomed had I not been the only black among a group of Lockheed employees who frequented the premises. I knew that a group of blacks either would have been ignored in hopes that they would leave, or would have received such poor service that they would not have returned. At least in Atlanta I was being told up front that I would not be welcome.

I was also told that travel would be required; but since I was in school, most of that travel could be accomplished over the weekend and on Monday when I had no classes. I would be required to work at least twenty hours per week, but I could work as many hours as my time permitted. Because I would be paid on an hourly basis but would be working in a salaried position, I was requested not to count travel time even though legally I could have. Elated to have found a challenging part-time position, I agreed to all of the conditions and became a Burroughs systems representative.

During the first few weeks of my employment, I was so busy learning the assembler code that I did not have time to reflect on the many stares I noticed I was receiving. Most of the women were clerical (as were the majority of working women in the South), and they resented the fact that I was a professional. Though I only worked full days on Monday, no one ever invited me to go to lunch. Generally, the women either did not like me, were jealous of me, or thought that I was interested in some of the white men in the office; most of the men would have felt uncomfortable going to lunch with a black woman. Everything was complicated by the fact that we would have been limited to Davis Brothers Cafeteria. I understood that this was probably expecting too much of white Southerners, so I quietly ate and worked alone.

Everyone spoke to me, smiled, and watched to see whether or not I could really do the job for which I had been hired. As soon as I had translated the programs into the Burroughs code, I was ready to test them on the computer. Because of insufficient computer hardware in the Atlanta district office, I had to go to the Burroughs Detroit headquarters for the test runs. I left as soon as I had completed my Friday classes, and spent the weekend and Monday in the Detroit computer room. I was glad to discover that I was not quite the novelty to the Detroit personnel that I was to Atlanta. The Detroit office had other black professionals (male), and I was accepted.

During the time that I worked in Detroit, I stayed in a hotel within walking distance of the office, and some of the staff invited me to lunch. I was glad that we could eat in any restaurant we chose, for having to worry about being refused service did not sit well with me. I pretended that not being included with the other employees in Atlanta did not bother me, but it did. It felt good to be invited and included and not reminded that skin color makes a difference. After several such trips to Detroit, my project was successfully completed. With this success I earned some respect in the Atlanta office. My manager was praised for having taken the risk of hiring me, and my peers started talking to me and asking me technical questions. As I overheard the conversations, I knew that the risk of which they were speaking was in hiring a black, not a person who did not know Burroughs assembler. The latter, not the former, was in my estimation a legitimate cause for concern. Suddenly I had become a knowledgeable employee, and the completion of my project meant new business for Burroughs. I noticed a decided change in attitude toward me. I was no longer just an ambitious black graduate student who had talked her way into a job for which she surely was not qualified, but I was one of that rare breed of intelligent blacks who was actually competent. Again I had become special, different from other blacks, for obviously not just any black could have successfully completed the project, only their black.

In order to work at least twenty hours per week, I always worked on Saturdays. Because the office was relatively empty on the weekend, co-workers who happened to be there were provided with the perfect opportunity to speak with me in privacy. Often I was asked, "How does everyone treat you?" "Who is prejudiced?" "Is there anyone who doesn't even speak to you?" These questions were usually followed with a discussion of the "best friend" who happened to be black; therefore, they personally did not have any problems with or prejudices toward me. These conversations always made me uncomfortable. Where were these liberal people with black friends when everyone else was staring at me and no one was inviting me to go to lunch? Most of the time these were one-way conversations with me as the listener, for I did not trust myself to respond. Before the co-worker returned to his desk, he would say something like, "Just ignore those who don't like you, and hang in there. I always knew you could do it!" It was easy to be supportive of one individual black who had proven herself, but even that was done in privacy. I wonder whether or not these conversations would have taken place had I failed with my initial project. And although words of encouragement were offered, I still was not invited to lunch or to anyone's home or to anything social. For the most part, I continued to work in relative isolation. Unlike the situation at Lockheed in California, no one came to take pictures of me at my desk or to see whether or not I was being treated the same as were white systems representatives. The entire office staff knew that I was being treated differently, and in this case, different was not better.

There was one exception to my impartial treatment, a senior manager who worked in the Atlanta branch of our district office. He was a white, middle-aged Southern gentleman. One day he called me into his office and complimented me on the successful completion of my assignment. There was something in his smile and in the tone of his voice that made me realize that this conversation would involve more than praise for work. He extended his compliments to include my looks and personality. With this turn in the conversation, I knew I was in trouble. He explained that he was very familiar with the warmth and love that black women were capable of providing, having had black maids in his house for years. As he spoke, I envisioned these maids as mistresses, but a mistress probably has more status and benefits than are extended to maids. He continued by explaining how cold and indifferent the relationship between himself and his wife had become. He said that he could be very generous and helpful to a young black woman who would show him the warmth and love he wanted.

I was shocked, but I did not know whether to act as though I did not understand his implications or simply to refuse him. I responded, "I'll bet you could, and if I think of anyone who would fit the bill, I'll let you know." My previous experience in the work world had taught me that many managers approach female employees and that some females do advance that way, but I noticed a certain plantation mentality accompanying this particular proposition that frightened me. This man was not just approaching a female employee; he was approaching—and specifically wanted—a black one.

Black women slaves had traditionally serviced white men, and many were granted special privileges not only for themselves, but also for their families. I did not have a slave mentality, and I was insulted. I left his office, never mentioned the incident to anyone, and kept my distance from that manager. I smiled and spoke when I saw him, but he never saw warmth in my eyes, and he got the message. I was glad that he controlled neither my raises nor my assignments.

I have often wondered how a young black woman raised in the South and having a slave mentality would have responded. She might have decided that it would be so easy to allow herself to be used in order to advance her career. She might have thought that she would be fired if she refused his offer. Neither thought ever entered my mind. Even if being fired had, I am sure that I would have responded exactly as I did. I also have wondered what effect this proposition would have had on me had this been my first job in corporate America. What happens to young women who are approached on their very first job? Do they begin a pattern that follows them throughout their corporate careers? If they submit and are promoted, do they doubt their real ability to succeed without that type of submission? Here again I was grateful for the training that had taught me that I could succeed without special favors from anyone. As far as I know, the incident was kept secret. Remember that this was 1963 in the hometown of Dr. Martin

Luther King, Jr., and I am sure that that particular manager was not interested in the publicity a mere rumor of interracial sexual harassment could have caused.

Because my strength was in programming languages, I was asked to learn ALGOL (a scientific programming language whose name is derived from Algorithmic Language), the scientific programming language used on the Burroughs 5500 computer. That computer was to be installed at the Georgia Institute of Technology, and my new assignment would involve assisting the two white male systems representatives assigned to that account. Both males were Southerners, but they accepted their assignment to train me as a real challenge. My success at Georgia Tech would certainly look good on their records, for if they could train me to handle this account, they could train anyone.

This attitude was apparent while I was mastering the first few tasks, but later I noticed a change. White people who have never known black people as peers somehow think that there is a fundamental difference between black people and white people. They believe that blacks think differently, learn differently, respond differently, and that all of their actions must be different from those of other human beings. These two white men discovered that I thought, learned, responded, and acted as others would in a similar position. They also discovered that I learned just a little more rapidly then they had expected, but they immediately attributed that to my having a college degree. Neither of them had been to college. It was somewhat shocking to me to discover that so many white men held technical positions for which they had not been formally trained. Even though colleges were not, at that time, offering degrees in computer science, black people without college degrees were just not given the opportunity of on-the-job training for technical positions. I suppose that it was just generally believed blacks could not handle technical work.

I not only mastered my original assignment of learning the ALGOL programming language, but I also learned to operate the Burroughs 5500 computer and became an expert in trouble-shooting both hardware and software problems. My manager was so pleased with my progress that he reassigned my two white male counterparts, and I was left with sole responsibility for the Georgia Tech account.

I had to arrange my graduate courses so that I could spend at least some time each day at Tech. I was given an office in the computer center, and I posted my hours so that I could assist the students in debugging their programs and in isolating hardware problems. I went to the Burroughs office on Saturdays to check my mail and to pick up my expense and salary checks. Soon I felt more like I was working for Tech than for Burroughs.

I discovered that in many ways the college environment tended to be more tolerant than the corporate environment. I was not nearly the novelty or the subject of so many stares because both college students and faculty were accustomed to seeing people who were different. There were foreign students, visiting faculty, and flower children all around, and I was just another oddball. My ability to do my job was the key; and although many of the students were shocked to see me in an office in the computer center, as long as I could help them debug their programs, they really did not care what I looked like. There were very few, if any, black students at Tech in 1964, and I do not recall ever seeing any at the computer center.

One day the director of the computer center came to talk to me and told me about the many inquiries he had received concerning my position at Tech. Some wanted to know if I was a student, others wanted to know if I was an instructor, and still others just wondered who I was and why I was there. The director said that he loved to let them know that I could easily be either a graduate student or an instructor, but that I was actually the Burroughs systems representative in charge of the Tech account. He told me that I was a beautiful visual aid helping to refute stereotypes. Every time I saw the shock on the faces of those who entered my office looking for the Burroughs representative and discovering that I was it, I thought of the director's words.

The manager who had hired me and given me the title of "Miss Georgia Tech" became engaged to one of the few female systems representatives in the office. He called me into his office to tell me about his engagement and upcoming marriage. I offered my congratulations, but wondered why he wanted to tell me about it privately. Because he had always been open and honest with me, he explained that he wanted to extend a blanket invitation to all employees, but the particular church in which the wedding was to be held did not allow black worshipers. He wanted to know whether or not, if my schedule permitted, I would like to attend the wedding. If I would like to attend, he would seek special permission for me to enter that sanctuary. My jaw dropped. This was almost more than I could bear. I could not even imagine a church that would not allow me to enter its sanctuary! I could not believe that in 1964 in Atlanta, Georgia, the oasis of the South, I could not attend a wedding anywhere it was being held! What followers of Jesus Christ would actually bar worshipers from his house because of the color of their skin, or for that matter, any reason at all? The Jesus who had become my personal Savior was no respecter of persons. All were equal and worthy in his sight. How could white Christians discriminate? Were they really Christians at all? Did they even know the same Jesus that I did?

I closed my mouth and said that in order to eliminate confusion, I simply would not plan to attend the ceremony. I really did not want to enter a church where I had to have special permission. My manager apologized and explained that he was not from the South, did not understand Southern customs or prejudices, and had warned me of some of the prejudicial atrocities when he had hired me. Shortly after the wedding, he and his new bride moved to Washington, D.C.

Then I was faced with a new manager. I was somewhat apprehensive, but he proved to be nicer than the one who had hired me. He read my file, observed my successful completion of assignments, and told me that he would be glad when I completed my graduate degree so that I could begin to work and travel full-time. The traveling was especially important to him as there were several clients who needed to be taught the ALGOL programming language, and I had mastered it. However, traveling was difficult for me, for all of the Atlanta district clients were in the Southeast, and travel accommodations for black people were limited.

But this manager not only carefully planned my trips to coincide with my class schedule, he also personally flew to each city and visited each hotel to make sure that I would not face any unpleasant situations on the road. (Segregation was not only stupid and ridiculous, it was also costly.) There was one particular incident in which this practice saved both me and Burroughs a good deal of embarrassment.

I was scheduled to teach ALGOL to programmers from a company located in Pascagoula, Mississippi. On my manager's pre-trip to Pascagoula, he discovered that there was not one hotel in which I could stay, and neither he nor I was terribly thrilled about my going to Mississippi. So my manager decided to hold the class in the Burroughs Office in Mobile, Alabama. There was a nearby Holiday Inn in which I was welcome, and the fifty-mile drive gave the programmers an opportunity to think about the inconvenience that segregation and racism caused. The office workers often referred to this incident as the case of bringing the mountain to Mohammed!

4

Marriage + School + Work

‎◈

During May of 1964 as I approached the end of my first year both in graduate school and with Burroughs Corporation, I started to seriously date one of my fellow seminarians. It was his desire upon graduation to serve as pastor of a local congregation, and he was not nearly so concerned about my working in the corporate world as he was about my aspirations to work in the ministry. I explained that I was in seminary to learn to teach Sunday school professionally, not to learn to pastor a local church. Although there are many women who currently aspire to serve as local pastors, in 1964 they were rarely offered the opportunity by mainline denominations. But this was not my goal; and on my birthday in July, we became engaged to be married.

I did not have any personal relationships with my co-workers at Burroughs, but people noticed my engagement ring and asked me about my wedding plans. I suppose that the women were relieved that I would not be trying to date any of the white male co-workers, and the men knew that they would feel more comfortable working with a married black woman than with a single one (married women are safer). It did seem that everyone was more friendly, but in the euphoria of love the world seems more friendly. In contrast to my previous boss's wedding, the entire office expected to be invited to my wedding and knew that they would have no difficulty in gaining access to my church. While white churches were often off limits to black people, all black churches were open to whites. Perhaps because blacks are in the minority, they are more willing to welcome others to join them. Whites may be more interested in preserving their purity and status as the majority race and believe that fraternization may lead to assimilation. The Reverend Walter L. Kimbrough and I were married on December 20, 1964, with many of my co-workers in attendance. Anyone who had not attended would have been viewed as prejudiced, so attendance was a must. I often overhead the question, "Are you going to Margie's wedding?" The response was never simply, "Yes," but rather, "Aren't you?"

My boss was very much concerned that marriage would break my pattern of work, travel, and study, and he inquired as to whether my new husband was opposed to my traveling. The idea that a married woman might not only work but be required to travel was still novel, and there were real concerns. The white Southern males with whom I worked were quite chauvinistic, and they were sure that if my husband forbade my work or travel, then I would certainly obey. However, I assured him that my husband and I were in agreement and that my work schedule would continue as previously established. So, my boss personally continued to visit the clients and cities to which I was to travel, and I did not experience unusual incidents of racial or sexual discrimination. There were, of course, the same stares and shock, but then it was the unsettled sixties and I was traveling in the South. By this time, I had learned simply to ignore those who were disconcerted by my physical appearance.

I continued with my primary assignment at Georgia Tech, but I also taught new clients both the ALGOL Programming Language and the use of the Burroughs 5500 computer. One new Alabama business was in need of this training, and my boss knew that I was the best person to provide it. However, because of the Alabama location and my commitment to the Georgia Tech account, arrangements were made for me to teach the class at Georgia Tech. I spoke with the clients by telephone several times informing them as to where and when the class would take place. Although I did not know it at the time, the person with whom I spoke thought that I was the secretary of the man who would be providing the training. I do not have a Southern accent and I probably sounded like an administrative person who made arrangements with clients. The thought that I might be the instructor never entered their minds. Surely no woman was capable of teaching a class in either the use of the computer or the ALGOL programming language.

When the appointed day arrived, I walked into the classroom with the necessary manuals and found a group of very surprised white men. One of them, thinking I was either lost or had inadvertently wandered into the wrong room, asked if he could help me. I answered, ''No, but I can help you. I'm here to teach this class!'' All mouths opened simultaneously in disbelief, but I simply ignored their reaction and began to teach the class. Ignoring signs of shock certainly had become second nature; and I thought that after they had adjusted to the fact that I was a black woman, they would relax and concentrate on the material to be learned.

I was wrong. My being a black woman was just too much to overcome. They started asking me where I came from, if I really worked for Burroughs, if I really knew the material, and where the man was whose secretary they had spoken with when the class had been arranged. I explained that they had made the arrangements with me and that we were wasting precious time and had better get on with the business at hand. When that did not work, I finally told them bluntly, ''Close your mouths and pay attention because I intend to teach this class. I have other commitments at Tech later today, and I don't have time to wait until you adjust to who I am!'' From that point on I ignored their

stares and taught the class. By the time we took our first break,
they had decided that I actually was competent. This was just
another illustration of how blacks have to repeatedly prove their
competence. I just do not believe that either a white man or
woman would have had the same problems that I had with that
hardcore group of Alabamans.

That night my husband reminded me of the limited exposure
white men from small Alabama towns have to professional
black women. When I told him how they had warmed up to me
during the day, he warned me to keep in mind that they were
only being kind because I happened to have information they
needed. In any other setting, I would still be inferior, a nigger.
This response shocked me, for his view of things was so
different from mine. I had not grown up in the South; I had not
experienced the injustices of separate schools, water fountains,
and bathrooms; I had no idea that people had such deep-seated
feelings about racial differences and inferiorities. On many
occasions my husband said to me, "You think white people like
you, but don't you forget that they will never think that you are
as good as they are. You are still a nigger." I resented the fact
that he said it, but there would be many times during the years to
come that I would remember it!

Being married, and especially to a minister (one of the few
professions acceptable for black men in the South), made it
possible for me to be included in some of the social events
sponsored for Burroughs employees. Very few restaurants,
hotels, or clubs welcomed blacks, and I am sure that Burroughs
personnel did not think it necessary to go to the trouble of
booking any of those more liberal establishments when the one
black, part-time employee probably did not want to attend the
function anyway. But because I was married to someone whom
most of my co-workers had seen and of whom they approved, it
was easier to be included in company events. Whenever my
husband and I did attend, we stayed for a very brief time,

sensing the discomfort around us. Although in this small way I was included socially by the company in general, I still was not invited into any individual homes as I had been in California. It probably never crossed the minds of my co-workers.

One person who was very uncomfortable around us was the manager who had propositioned me. I am sure that he wondered whether or not I had told my husband about it, for my husband was much younger and much bigger than he was. Though he never said anything to me in the presence of my husband, he would often stop me in the office and ask whether my husband was being good to me. It did occur to me that he might have been restating his offer.

Over the years I have observed that sometimes married women are more inclined to become involved in an office dalliance. Married women know the ropes, are protected in case of pregnancy, and are less likely to be suspected by other co-workers. (An attractive single woman is always suspect.) My marital status did make me less apprehensive about talking with the manager, for I knew that I could always threaten to tell my husband. It is amazing how married women tend to use their husbands for protection against unwanted advances and then use them as a shield when participating in solicited affairs. Throughout the remainder of my tenure with Burroughs, that manager always had a certain gleam in his eyes, but he never again overtly approached me.

I continued in the same pattern of working after classes and on Mondays, traveling on weekends and during breaks from classes, and adjusting to being married. I was successful on all accounts, and in May of 1965 I graduated at the top of my class receiving my Master of Christian Education degree summa cum laude. Again I had performed as expected, ahead of all the rest.

Then I started working and traveling full-time. I continued to staff the Georgia Tech account, establishing full-day schedules when there were no classes to be taught out of town. Both my

responsibilities and my pay had increased; however, there was
no discussion of change in title or the assumption of supervisory
duties. I suppose that having a black woman supervise white
men was unthinkable and therefore unmentioned.

However, when Burroughs decided to follow IBM's lead and
use the COBOL (a business programming language whose
name is derived from Common Business Oriented Language)
on its new 2000 series computers, I was selected to be the one to
first learn the language and then teach all of the other systems
representatives. It was conceded that I learned more quickly
than the others and had better communication skills. So, after a
full day at Georgia Tech, I went to the Burroughs Office to teach
a group of equally tired systems representatives who had also
put in a full day. I knew that there was some resentment
accompanying the fact that I had been selected to teach. After
all, this did put a black woman in the position of teaching her
peers, and it suggested that she was perhaps a bit more
competent than they were. This situation was further
complicated by the fact that I was simply staying one lesson
ahead of the class. We all had received the COBOL manuals at
the same time, and none of us had had previous exposure to the
new language. Again the confidence that had been instilled in
me as a child paid off, for I knew that if anyone could learn the
material and teach it, I could. I did have an aptitude for higher
level languages; and since I already knew both FORTRAN and
ALGOL, COBOL—being less scientific and more like business
English—was easy. So I learned it and taught it, and along the
way, I even earned the respect of some of my peers.

Early in 1966 my husband and I had to come to terms with our
separate careers and his impending graduation from seminary.
He had several offers from churches in different parts of the
country, and it was important for us to decide whose career
would dictate our relocation. At that time, churches that paid
livable salaries were few and far between, especially for young

black seminarians. We decided that we should accept his best offer, regardless of the location. I knew that my data processing skills were very marketable, and I assumed that if I had found a job in the South, I could find one anywhere. As I later experienced the more subtle forms of Northern racism, I recalled the error of that assumption.

Many researchers say that a woman who decides to allow her husband's career to dictate the family's relocation plans will never succeed in her own career.[1] Some women are willing to sacrifice their marriages for their careers. I was not. I knew my husband, and I knew that he needed me to support his decisions for the two of us as a family. He promised always to consult me in making important decisions, but he asked me to let the final decision be his. I agreed, for I knew that he felt responsible for me and that he would be there for me when my career was not. I do not apologize for my acquiescence: at this writing I have been happily married for twenty-six years, and I would not change my actions.

My husband's best offer was in Chicago. He had never lived outside Atlanta and was very excited about the opportunities in the North. He would be the first black pastor serving a congregation in racial transition. I spoke with my boss about the move. He contacted the Burroughs Chicago office, but there were no openings. I contacted my previous boss who had moved to Washington, D.C. I knew that he was heading up a consulting firm and that he might know of some work I could do from a Chicago location. This proved to be a fruitful contact, for he did know of some consulting that would be available to me. So, after three years with Burroughs Corporation, two years of which I had worked part-time while obtaining both an MRS and an MRE, and one year working full-time, I moved to Chicago and began a career as an independent programming languages consultant.

1. Ann M. Morrison, Randall P. White, Ellen Van Velsor and the Center for Creative Leadership, "Women with Promise: Who Succeeds, Who Fails?" *Working Woman* (New York: Working Woman/McCall's Group, June, 1987), pp. 79-82.

5

Chicago

In 1966 Chicago was a city run by The Boss, Mayor Richard J. Daley. It was also a city in racial transition. Many neighborhoods were experiencing white flight—that is, whites were moving out faster than blacks were moving in. Having studied and worked most of my life in predominantly white environments, I had discovered that white people tend to flee as soon as they find themselves in the minority. One or two black people on the job or in the neighborhood is acceptable, but the presence of enough blacks to constitute the majority certainly is not. Unaccustomed to being in that position, most white people are uncomfortable as minorities.

Everyone who is young enough to negotiate a new mortgage in a predominantly white neighborhood moves. Thus, the new black neighborhood has only a few elderly white residents. The irony of this situation is that generally the black people moving in are more middle class than the white people who are moving out. On the other hand, the new neighborhoods to which many of the whites run are much poorer than the ones they have left. I always wondered why the white people never realized that if they did not sell, the blacks could not buy, and they would still have a predominantly white neighborhood.

As the neighborhood transits, so does the church. Somehow

all Christians have not learned that all of God's children are equal and precious in his sight. As soon as the majority of those in the church do not have the same complexion as do those in the minority, then relocation for those minority members is inevitable. If I adhered to this policy, then I would have to believe in one god who is many and differs for each racial group, not in one God who is all. So, as my husband and I moved into the church parsonage in which the white minister and his family had lived, we were stared at both by the neighbors and by the white church members. Many of the members announced that they would be moving their church memberships as soon as their houses were sold. I thought that this was most unchristian, but racism somehow transcends Christianity. Even Jesus could not convince everyone that all people are the same.

I tried to let my husband concentrate on the problems at the church while I concentrated on my new freelance consulting career. But the members did not like the fact that I was a minister's working wife. I was supposed to stay at home to fix covered dishes for church suppers, play the organ for church services, and volunteer as church secretary. I agreed to none of the above, and announced that I was a professional and intended to continue to work and travel. When that announcement received objections, I simply asked some of the sisters whether or not they went to work with their husbands. When they replied, "Of course not!" I said "And neither will I!"

Now this does not mean that I was not willing to work in the church and in every way possible help my husband succeed in his career. I just resented being dictated to by the congregation and assigned specific roles. I had always worked in the church, but like other members, I like to choose my position. I saw no reason to change just because I was the minister's wife.

Being a part of the predominantly white Rock River

Conference of the Methodist Church,[1] I was in a unique position. While the majority of the white wives did not work, the black wives did. However, their jobs did not require travel as most were public school teachers. The fact that I was black, working, and traveling was very hard for the white members and most of the black ones to accept. But I was determined to have my own career, and I did not allow their disfavor to distract me.

My contact in Washington, D.C. (the person for whom I had previously worked at Burroughs), requested that I learn a new programming language so that I could design and teach a course on comparative programming languages. This particular new language had been introduced by IBM as their new scientific programming language, PL1, a combination of ALGOL and FORTRAN. Since I already knew both ALGOL and FORTRAN, PL1 (whose name is derived from Programming Language One) had to be easy.

I was sent the manuals and books, learned PL1, and designed a one-week course comparing the four higher level languages, FORTRAN, ALGOL, PL1, and COBOL. I wrote an accompanying textbook, and the course was offered as a one-week seminar in major cities across the nation. I usually left home after church on Sunday and returned on Friday night. My husband unintentionally made my departure more noticeable by announcing from the pulpit on Sundays that I would be out of town that week and he would like to have dinner invitations to cover each night! Whispers abounded that this minister's horrible wife left her husband to beg for dinner among his congregation. The real truth was that my husband hated to eat alone, and he used this time for home visitations. He felt that this programming of his time was quite creative, but the congregation misunderstood and used my traveling to support

---

1. The name of this conference has since been changed to the Northern Illinois Conference of The United Methodist Church.

their belief that the minister's wife should stay at home and have her husband's dinner ready whenever he returned from attending to their spiritual needs.

This was a difficult time for me. I certainly did not want to hinder my husband's career in any way, and I knew he had quite enough to deal with without any rumblings about his wife. I had to rely on my inner resources, my belief in prayer, and on Mama's constant admonition to "let go and let God." This gave me the confidence that I could convince the congregation to accept me as I was and to respect me as a professional. The fact that I had always been active in the church teaching Sunday school and working with the youth group did help. Soon the members decided that although I was different from what they had known and expected, I was not a heathen and that I did on occasion actually accomplish some good works.

During this period of time, my husband had no comment. He knew that I wanted to work, and he knew that he needed for me to work as starting salaries for ministers were just above the poverty level. So he just let me work it out. He knew that once the members got to know me and appreciate my talent everything would be fine. And it was. All of us grew as a result of having to adjust to changing times and roles for both men and women. I thank God for it!

Thus I began to teach my newly designed seminar on programming languages. The seminars that I taught were held in major hotels across the country, and because of previous travel experiences, no Southern cities were included.

Upon checking in to these hotels, I was always viewed with some skepticism, but I tried to maintain an air of professionalism. Sometimes I was greeted with, "I'm sorry, Mrs. Kimbrough, but we do not have a reservation for you." I would simply ask whether or not a seminar on programming languages was scheduled to be held there that week. When the response was affirmative, I would say, "Isn't it interesting that my company managed to book the seminar and not the instructor's reservation? I guess I will have to tell them never to use this hotel again.'' Miraculously, my reservation always materialized.

But why this response? When a clerk looked at the black woman before him, did he not believe that I could afford the room, think I should not be staying in the hotel, or just want to inconvenience me? Now, I do know that every business traveler's hotel reservations have been lost on occasion, but not with the frequency I experienced. I did notice, however, that once I had had a personal encounter with a particular hotel *clerk,* I never had future difficulties with that particular *hotel.* I am sure that each subsequent clerk was forewarned of my coming.

On Monday mornings I had to arrange to have the manuals I had written delivered to the meeting room. All other arrangements had been taken care of by the Washington office. So with the logistics taken care of, I walked into the room, introduced myself as the instructor, welcomed the participants, and started to teach the class. All of the participants had registered in response to flyers that announced the seminar, included a brief synopsis, and provided my name as instructor along with a biographical sketch. The class, composed almost exclusively of white males, did expect a female named Marjorie Kimbrough as its instructor, they just did not expect a black female. There is nothing about my name or my educational background that would reveal my race. But I was well accustomed to the shocked looks.

Generally, there were lots of questions during the first half of the morning. I am sure that my competence was being challenged. It probably would have been comforting to some attendees to be able to say that they had uncovered my incompetence and all monies should be refunded. They were unfamiliar with my personal history that had instilled within me the philosophy of never attempting a project unprepared. I always answered their questions, taught with a friendly ease (I enjoy teaching), and received glowing written comments at the end of the seminar.

The participants ate lunch together as lunch was included in the seminar fee, but I was never invited to drinks or dinner after class. Some of the men did get together, but I was accustomed to their feeling uncomfortable with including me. Once or twice I tried eating in the hotel restaurant alone, but I was approached by some business man who thought I wanted to be picked up. A single woman dining alone was considered fair game for those interested in "having a little fun." As a result, I usually went to my room after class, called my husband, and ordered room service.

My Washington, D.C., employer was very pleased with the response the seminar was getting, and he encouraged me to attend updates on the programming languages that I was teaching. As the need arose, I, in turn, updated my textbook, and additional cities were selected as future seminar sites. The schedule of presenting one seminar per month worked perfectly for me as it provided me with sufficient time at home to take care of the parsonage and work in the church. I even had time to participate actively with the ministers' wives and found that group of women to be very supportive.

Some of the ministers' wives, most of whom were white, found my career as shocking as had our members. Many expressed the feeling that their husbands would never permit them to travel. They also wondered how I would manage when I had children. Yet, I could see the envy in their eyes, and I knew that many of them felt somewhat limited by their own career choices or lack of career involvement outside the church and home. At this writing, almost all ministers' wives are employed outside the home. Meetings that were once held in the middle of the day are now held in the evenings or on Saturday. The workforce has certainly changed, and ministers' wives are a part of that change. They no longer want to be the church secretary or the church organist. They want independent careers and independent recognition, the things I always wanted.

This career issue is even more critical for the wives of United Methodist ministers. United Methodist ministers are assigned to their churches, or appointments as they are called, for one year at a time. When reappointment occurs, it may be to a different church in a different city or state. It was expected that the wife would quit her job, losing any tenure or seniority she had accumulated, and move with her husband to his new appointment. This is probably why so many wives simply worked part-time at the church with their husbands. In this way, the congregation got two workers for the price of one, and moving and finding a new job for the wife was much less complicated.

Increasingly, as the time for reappointment approached, working wives wondered whether they should quit their jobs, which often paid more than their husband's church. Some even decided to let their husbands move alone, and some divorced. Because my traveling could be done from any major city, my job was very attractive to all of the wives. More than twenty years later, this issue is still of major concern to many United Methodist ministers' spouses.

I continued to meet and support these ministers' wives as I maintained my schedule of teaching seminars, attending update classes, and revising my textbook. Near the end of 1966, I called my supervisor to let him know that I would not be available to teach the Spring seminars as I was expecting my first child in April. He congratulated me and advised me that I could travel through February, my seventh month, and that we would begin to make arrangements for a baby-sitter as soon as I was able to travel after the birth.

I suppose that I had resigned myself to the fact that the

traveling would have to cease with a newborn. In fact my husband had asked me not to leave the baby until he was at least one year old. He did say 'he,' for my husband never doubted that we would have a boy. I had never considered the possibility of hiring a baby-sitter to take care of the baby in the hotel in which I was working. But my supervisor informed me that there were licensed and bonded sitters, many of whom were retired nurses, in all of the cities to which I traveled.

I discussed this with my husband, and he agreed that we should explore the possibilities. If I was satisfied with the baby-sitting agencies and if the cost was not prohibitive, then I could continue to travel taking the baby with me. Some people will undoubtedly think that this should have been my decision and not his; however, I had agreed not to leave the baby before he was one year old, and taking him with me would not constitute leaving him. This to me was a most affable arrangement.

My supervisor provided names of the agencies and told me that his company would assume the expense. I was pleased with the results obtained from my investigation of the agencies, and I was thrilled that the expenses would be taken care of for me. At that time the cost was approximately twenty-five dollars a day for the sitter, and I was making two hundred dollars a day. I was told to pay the sitter at the end of the week and then include the item with my other expenses. I would be reimbursed for the sitter along with the reimbursement of my other expenses.

Thus, having solved the dilemma of what to do after the baby was born, I continued with my previously established schedule. As my pregnancy became visible, my seminar participants became more uncomfortable. It was as though they were saying, "It's bad enough to be taught by a black female, but this pregnancy just adds insult to injury."

Again, it was up to me to help them overcome this added distraction. It seemed that I was always having to make people forget me and concentrate on learning the material at hand. I tried to reassure them that I had taught the course many times before and that the baby was not due for quite some time, so they had nothing to worry about except the seminar.

In February, 1967, during my final seminar before the birth, I was approached by a participant who said that his company was looking for someone to write a programmed instruction textbook on PL1. He knew that I had written the text that we were using in the seminar, and he felt that I could write the text his company needed. I gave him my address, and he said that I would be contacted within the next week.

When I was contacted by the Texas firm that the participant represented, both of us were pressed for time. The firm needed the text to train its new PL1 programmers who were being hired in the spring to complete a project that was due in the fall. There were no instructors in place who could train these programmers, and a programmed instruction text seemed to be a viable alternative. A programmed instruction textbook is a self-learning text that provides sample exercises and answers to assist in learning the subject matter at hand. I had never written such a text before, but I had seen one and used one to learn COBOL when I was working for Burroughs.

The confidence that I was equal to the task was with me, and I asked how long I had to complete the project and how much money I would be paid. I was told that I would have two months to complete the project and I would be paid $3,000. There would be a project team to check the accuracy of my instruction text, and I would receive the money as soon as my work had been approved. I signed a contact to that effect, and I looked at the calendar. I had exactly two months before my due date. Knowing then that my due date had a double meaning, I worked especially hard to complete the project. I sent in sample chapters for approval along the way, and with the confidence that my work was acceptable, I finished the text the day before my water broke. How is that for perfect timing?

6

Babies

I t was not an easy labor. After several hours, I was making no progress toward delivery. Finally the doctor decided to deliver by Cesarean section. So it was that on April 22, 1967, our first child, a son, Walter Mark Kimbrough, was born. My husband was right; it was a boy. And it is a good thing that it was, for my husband had boldly announced to the congregation the Sunday prior to the birth that I would not be in church but in the hospital with our son on the following Sunday.

The Cesarean section extended my period of convalescence and consequently extended the time before I could proceed with my plans to travel with the baby. My Washington, D.C., supervisor called while I was still in the hospital, and I told him that I preferred not to travel until late summer or early fall. He informed me that my timing was perfect because his company was withdrawing from the seminar business; however, the University Computing Company (UCC) in Dallas, Texas, was interested in sponsoring my seminar. By the time I was ready to travel, UCC would be ready to hire me, on a consulting basis, as one of their seminar instructors.

I was somewhat uneasy about this announcement, for I was afraid a new company might not pay for the baby-sitter, or even agree to my traveling with the baby. I thanked him for making the contacts for me, and I decided to deal with the whole situation when the time came. At worst I could find a job that did not require travel.

I never really heard from that supervisor again, for his company began to specialize in economic and industrial research, and there was no reason for him to contact me. Although he had been a concerned manager—one who takes care of employees who produce for the business—he had never become a personal friend. That was also true of most of my business contacts. Somehow the white people with whom I worked were cordial at work, but distant personally and socially. Nevertheless, my former manager was true to his word, and a UCC representative contacted me with regard to conducting the programming languages seminar for his company.

I requested the latest published materials on the languages, updated my textbook, and discussed the cities to which I was willing to travel. This time I was more interested in whether there were licensed and bonded baby-sitters in the city than whether I would face discrimination. After having worked and traveled for several years, I felt that I could handle the discrimination, but I did not want to have to worry about the care of my baby while I was teaching a seminar. If I were traveling today, I would also have to be concerned about the issues of child abuse that have become much more prevalent in recent years. I probably would not be as willing to leave my child with a stranger even if that stranger were licensed and bonded.

I agreed to four seminars that fall, and I checked each location carefully for a reputable baby-sitting agency. I arranged to meet each sitter prior to the seminar (the Sunday night I arrived), and I was given references and tremendous reassurance. My previous experience with shocked expressions made it important for me to see the sitter and to make sure that she was well aware that she would be caring for a black child. The fact that the agency was licensed and bonded would only give me the right to sue if my child were abused, but I did not want an abused child.

I always felt much better once I had met and talked with the sitter. Many of the white sitters were retired nurses, and most of the black ones, though usually not trained as nurses, were just good women who loved children. Once I had established rapport with a particular sitter, I always requested her for the next seminar in that city.

I packed disposable diapers, baby food, an electric baby dish (in which I could heat the baby food), and I requested a crib in my hotel room. Most good hotels do not charge for infants or cribs in the room; and, of course, there was no additional air fare. Upon arrival I ordered milk from room service, filled the ice bucket (which I used to keep the milk cold), and prepared to meet the sitter with whom I would be working for the rest of the week.

The sitters were always afraid that my child would cry and scream when I left the room for my seminar, but traveling with me had taught my son that I would return by the end of the day. I have observed that many children who cry for extended periods when faced with parental separation fear that the parent will never return. Additionally, having met the sitter previously in my presence provided my child with a certain sense of security. In fact one sitter who was concerned that my child was too calm during my absence decided to bring him to my seminar room during the lunch break just to ask me if he was all right. Seeing me in those unusual surroundings and sensing the nervousness of the sitter did upset him, and that is the only time that I remember his having cried when leaving me.

For the most part, those wonderful sitters are to be commended for their resourcefulness. They did not just entertain the child in the hotel room. They took him out to the park, and depending upon the city and his age, he was taken on various tours and outings. As he grew older, in Washington, D.C., he toured the White House, in New York, he rode the Staten Island Ferry and visited the Statue of Liberty, and in Seattle, he visited Puget Sound.

One of my favorite sitters in Washington, D.C., even invited him to go trick-or-treating with her children on Halloween. Although my son was young, he enjoyed being with the other children, and I was glad that he did not have to miss all of the fun of Halloween just because he was traveling with his mother.

The sitters always saved the visits to the nearby downtown department stores for me, so that I could buy him something for being so good while I was working. Incidentally, this child, currently a graduate student, is extremely well adjusted, has excelled in school, and did not suffer at all from my having worked immediately before and after his birth. In fact he has continued to travel extensively, having already gone to Europe three times with academic and extracurricular activities.

My seminar participants could not believe that I actually had a baby with me on these trips. Most of the men felt that their wives could not have handled this kind of adventure. But I knew that this, too, was another way of making me the exception, the black woman who was different and therefore acceptable to them. Again, I became their special black person, the one who could be recommended to others because she was not like any of the others they had met.

The seminars continued to be popular throughout 1967, 1968, and most of 1969. I never personally met my employer at UCC. All arrangements were handled through the mail. I sent in the updates to my material; the material was reprinted for me by UCC; the material was sent to the respective hotels from Dallas; I sent in my expense reports after each seminar; and my checks were mailed to my home in Chicago.

There was one thing about which the accountant raised objections—the twenty-five dollar a day baby-sitting fee. He complained that he had no way to account for that expense on his books, and he asked that the additional monies be included in my consultant fee. My fee was increased fifty dollars a day to cover both any increase in child care expenses and/or in taxes due to higher personal income.

I continued to work and travel with my son through the seventh month of my second pregnancy. This pregnancy complicated things somewhat as I tired more easily and had to deal with a two-year-old after having taught all day. One trip to Washington, D.C., was particularly stressful. I arrived late one Sunday night carrying my two-year-old and being very visibly pregnant. The desk clerk greeted me with the fact that I did not have a reservation. I was clearly not in the mood to play that old, worn out game.

I simply told the clerk that I was in the right hotel, I did have a seminar there the next day, I was meeting my sitter there later that night, and I was not leaving. I further told him that I was going to sit in the lobby until they found me a room. I also let him know that my baby was tired and would soon start crying and that if I was sufficiently upset, I just might even go into labor.

In very short order a bellman came to escort me to my room. He said, "Someone won't have a room here tonight, but it isn't going to be you!" The hotel may legitimately have been overbooked, but after my many experiences with the same scenario, I just was not willing to make any adjustments. I am sure that my manner and tone of voice indicated as much!

During one of my seminars while I was carrying my second child, a participant asked if I was Cuban. (At that time the United States and Cuba were involved in quite a few discussions, and I suppose that is why Cuba came to mind.) I could not understand why my nationality was significant, so I asked him why he wanted to know. He said that he had never known a black person who knew anything about computers, and that a pregnant black woman was just more than he could handle. Being Cuban would at least have been a step above being black, and therefore more acceptable to him.

I did not usually tell people that I was originally from Mississippi, but this time I did. I wanted him to visualize the most poverty-stricken, poor, uneducated black person and know that this person was teaching him. Being from California or Chicago would have been too progressive and therefore easier to accept. I wanted him to know that my roots were in the poor South and that I was an ordinary black woman, married, pregnant, and traveling with another child.

Somehow immigrants are more acceptable to the white business community than are blacks who were born in this country. Blacks never quite fit into the mainstream of American life. There are only a few exceptions, and those are the special people—the ''best friends'' that every white person has. Although it was true that the United States and Cuba were frequently mentioned together in the news during this period of time, there was no way that I could have been mistaken for a Cuban. This was just another form of racism, another of the corporate encounters with which I had to deal.

On October 1, 1969, our second son, Wayne Martin Kimbrough, was born. This time I was expecting the Cesarean delivery and the period of convalescence. I used the time to decide how I would continue to work with two small children. I knew that I could not allow my two-year-old to feel rejected because I had left him at home while I took the new baby with me on my business trips. And I knew that I could not leave the new baby at home while I continued to travel with the older one. My husband's feelings about not leaving a child during the first year still applied, and I summoned all of my resources to come up with a new working arrangement. So I told my representative at UCC that I would no longer be available to teach the seminar, updated my résumé, and started to look for a part-time position that did not involve traveling. The need to continue to work was especially important to me because of the data processing industry. I knew how rapidly it was changing and I felt that if I stayed away from it too long, my knowledge would be obsolete by the time I decided to return. I went to a couple of agencies that specialized in placing data processing personnel, and was faced with the fact that my credentials were viewed with some degree of skepticism.

I was told by one recruiter, "I see, Marjorie, that you are a black girl who is accustomed to making a lot of money, and I want you to know that you just won't find that much money for your kind in Chicago." I wanted to ask him what my kind was, but I did not because I already knew. Another recruiter asked if I would be interested in continuing to teach programming languages. Of course I said that I would, but that I could not travel. He informed me of a company in the Chicago area that produced video tapes to be used in data processing instruction. The concept of video-assisted instruction was relatively new in 1969, and this recruiter felt that I would project well on tape. He scheduled an interview for me with Advanced Systems, Inc. I must applaud this recruiter's courage in recommending me, for he could not know whether Advanced Systems would be willing to send a tape of a black woman to their clients. Could white men really learn from a black woman teaching computer concepts?

At that time Advanced Systems, Inc. was located in Mount Prospect, Illinois, a rather prosperous, white Chicago suburb. I took my résumé, copies of the textbooks I had written, and went to meet the interviewer. As with many small companies involved in some aspect of data processing, there was no formal personnel department. The senior managers of the company did both the interviewing and the hiring.

I was interviewed by a manager and an instructor. The manager asked general questions, and the instructor evaluated the accuracy of my responses. The instructor also explained the procedures involved in making video-assisted instruction tapes. Each course was to be taught within a predetermined number of tapes or lessons. I would design each tape, teach it on camera, and write an accompanying textbook to be used along with the tapes. In fact, at some points during the tape, the student would be instructed to turn off the tape and complete designated exercises in the written text.

There was general agreement that I was qualified to teach the courses for which an instructor was needed. It was also agreed that my communication skills and experience in teaching live seminars enhanced my qualifications. My having minored in speech at the University of California and my Master's degree in Christian Education certainly did not hurt. The only problem was that I was black and there had never been a black instructor. The manager was not sure the salesmen would be able to sell a tape featuring a black instructor. Racism was alive and well in Chicago and its surrounding suburbs.

By this time I was familiar with these objections. They are often stated diplomatically, but they all amount to the same thing. So I asked to make a test tape to be shown to the salesmen. We went to the studio and I gave a brief introduction to FORTRAN, one of the languages with which I was intimately familiar. Fortunately, I photograph well, my diction is precise, and I am very much at ease in front of the camera. Both the manager and the instructor loved my tape, and the decision was made to hire me. The manager said that he would be responsible for selling me to the salesmen, and he appointed the instructor who had been in the interview with us as my supervisor. Again, the confidence that Mama had instilled helped me to earn the position; however, the potential for increasing sales that the manager could see in my ability was what sealed the bargain. Racism is powerful, but not as powerful as the almighty dollar! If you can increase the bottom-line profits, you can be purple, but you have to be given the opportunity. Racism often restricts the opportunity.

I had found the perfect job. I designed my tapes and wrote the accompanying text at home, then I went to the studio for the taping. This meant that I was at home every day some weeks, and I was at the studio every day other weeks. I enrolled my older son in a nearby nursery school and hired one of the retired members of our congregation to keep the baby in my home on the days I had to go to the studio. Thus, I was both at home and working at the same time.

Being in touch with a company also provided me with the opportunity to go to an office and interact with business people in a peer rather than student-teacher relationship. Again though, there were only polite "hello's" with no real, personal interaction. But I was busy and usually trying to complete a tape and then get back home to my family. Most of the time I did not take a lunch break or stay around for drinks after work. I sensed that my being unavailable for personal relationships did not particularly disturb anyone, and I would not allow it to disturb me. I did establish a rather friendly relationship at the office with the cameramen and technicians. They thought that I was exceptional on tape and very interesting to watch. I enjoyed doing it, and it showed.

I was paid as each tape was completed and approved for release by my supervisor. After the first tape was completed, a portion of it was shown at the sales meeting. The manager who had hired me used my work to sell me to the salesforce in much the same way that I had used my work to sell myself to him. The salesmen were excited about the new course, and for many years to come I met people throughout the nation who had learned a programming language from my video-assisted instruction courses.

I not only designed, wrote, and taught my own courses, but also taught some courses that others designed and wrote. Some people did not project well on camera, so I learned their material and taught their courses. Initially there was some objection by the other instructors to my teaching their material, but once they were paid the objections ceased. It must also be noted that working on camera is tedious and some of the instructors, in addition to not being very good at it, did not enjoy doing it.

Some of the objections were rooted in the fact that I was black and starring before the cameras while some of the real authors of the material were hidden in the background. A white presenter would have been more palatable, but I was available and prided myself on doing a good job. Again, that old home training of being better than the rest was still real in my life, and it paid off.

In a way I was still teaching my seminars. I was just going to the studio to tape, and the tapes were being sent to different cities while I stayed at home. I did not feel as though I was really working for a company, as I was in a consulting relationship. I never attended a company function, and I never interacted with company employees. Although I did physically see my employers at Advanced Systems, I had no more relationship with them than I had had with the people at UCC in Dallas.

I taught on video tape for two years, and then my husband decided it was time to return to Atlanta. Our older son was ready to begin public school, and our younger son was old enough for nursery school. All of these developments contributed to my belief that I was ready to go back to work on a full-time basis.

7

Teaching Graduate School

∾

I felt that with the move to Atlanta, I was ready to return to corporate America on a full-time basis, but the past several years had taught me caution. I wanted to find both a company with which I could grow and a position that would not only fully utilize my existing skills, but also provide opportunities for the development of new ones. I knew that finding the right position would not be easy, so I decided to take my time.

While my husband was busy getting settled in his new pastoral appointment and we were all settling into our new parsonage, I enrolled my older son in public school and my younger one in nursery school. Then I started looking at available data processing positions. I decided to consult a recruitment agency in order to develop a current view of the Atlanta job market for data processing professionals.

During this period of decision making, the president of the Interdenominational Theological Center (which is a part of the Atlanta University Complex) informed me that he needed an instructor for two courses in Christian education. Accepting this position would provide some income while still allowing me time to look for a full-time position in data processing. So I signed a contract for the 1972–1973 school year.

Both of the courses that I was scheduled to teach, Teaching

Christian Education to Adults and Teaching Christian Education to Children, were held in the morning, leaving my afternoons free to look for a data processing position. I arranged conferences with my students between classes, and I was able not only to be at home when my older son came home from kindergarten, but also to pick up my younger one from nursery school.

Because I had always enjoyed teaching, working on the graduate school level was enjoyable. By the time most adults reach graduate school, they are serious about learning. Enrolling in seminary was strictly an individual choice, and the students either did the assigned work, or they were dismissed.

Although the seminary was predominantly black, it was both interdenominational and international. I had never really taught black adults on a professional level before, for most of the adults whom I had taught in the data processing industry were white, and I found this experience to be enlightening. The classes were composed primarily of men who were preparing for the ministry, and most of the other instructors were not only male, but also ordained ministers. Therefore, the whole teaching-learning atmosphere was different from that found in the corporate business environment.

Because my husband was a minister and I was very active in the church, many of the students felt that I could relate to and understand the problems they would have to face in their ministries. This vote of confidence was never extended to me when I taught in the business world. In the first place, most of the white men I taught could not even imagine my having faced any of the problems they were facing on their jobs. In the second place, it would not have occurred to them to seek the advice and counsel of a black woman. And, in the third place, they were so busy trying either to accept me or to prove my incompetence that they did not have time to do anything except grasp the material being taught. And sometimes they found it impossible to do that very well.

But teaching a class composed predominantly of black males changed all of that. I was much more aware of my being female, and I actually felt attractive—not just different. I appreciated the smiles and admiring glances, for I was no longer afraid of them. In previous working situations there had been that nagging, perhaps subconscious feeling that this white man's intentions are not honorable and I must be on guard. This same thought probably could have been in my mind as I dealt with black men, but I felt, under these particular circumstances, surrounded by ministers, that their divine calling rather than their base natures would prevail. I was not mistaken.

After many years of working in a somewhat isolated and lonely environment, I finally had the opportunity to socialize, on a regular basis, with both my co-workers and with the students. There were lunches, evening dinners, socials for faculty and students, and other activities that provided a family atmosphere. I had not had that experience in any of my previous positions. I must admit that it was a welcome change, but somehow I knew that I could not retreat permanently within this more comfortable atmosphere. Had I decided to continue teaching, I would have sought a doctoral degree and my data processing skills would have been lost. And, although I enjoyed what I was doing, I felt that many others could have done it. When I was working in the corporate world, I had felt that I was fulfilling a ministry that was mine alone. While today there are many black women both in corporate America and particularly in data processing, at that time I seemed to be the only one. Therefore, responding to my unique ministry was important to me.

And that ministry did call me. I wanted white men to have to deal with my black face and my level of expertise. I wanted them to be shocked when I confronted them, and I wanted to travel again. Teaching in a small graduate school was not big enough for what I considered my mission to be. I knew that both Atlanta and the South were not the same in 1972 as they had been in 1966 when I had moved to Chicago. There were more places where blacks could eat and stay, and there were more jobs in which blacks could and were being employed. But there were still doors to be opened, and somehow I knew that there was one special job waiting for me. I set out to find it.

I went back to Burroughs, the company I had left in 1966. The office had been relocated and most of the employees I had known were no longer there. I asked about the type of openings available, but these jobs did not lead in the direction I wanted to move. I knew that I wanted to concentrate on the COBOL Programming Language, for the business world was moving exclusively toward COBOL. I also wanted to work directly with customers. And, because I had made a relatively good salary working part-time, I wanted an excellent full-time salary.

Seeing no COBOL advertisements for which I felt qualified, I responded to an advertisement for a FORTRAN Department Programming Manager at Georgia State University. I was tested for both FORTRAN and management skills. I was told that it had not been expected that a black woman would qualify for the position, but the university was an equal opportunity employer and, if I wanted it, I could have the job. Almost in the same breath, I was also told that there were no other black managers and that most of the programmers in the department had never worked for a black person before. In other words, I was told to expect problems. I asked for time to think about it.

I was hesitant to accept this offer. I really did not want to concentrate on FORTRAN programming when the whole data processing industry, and thus its associated job market, was moving toward COBOL. The position also seemed somewhat confining. There was no travel and very little interaction with anyone other than the small group of programmers being managed. I was not sure that I could grow sufficiently in this position, and I was looking for a company with which I could stay for a long time.

I had sent out several other résumés, and I had received some rejection letters. I called the recruiter with whom I had been working and told him about the Georgia State offer. I also told him about my reservations and described the type of position I really wanted. He responded by telling me about a software company that was reorganizing after bankruptcy and said that he could arrange an interview. When he named the company, I told him that I had already sent them a résumé and had been rejected.

He insisted that I had the right qualifications for the positions being filled and told me to come in so that he could help me rewrite my résumé. I did that, and he sent in my résumé with a cover letter from his agency. (He did not mention the fact that I had already been rejected.) This time I was invited to come in for an interview.

Because there were very few changes in my résumé, I would guess that my being recommended by an agency with which the company had done previous business got me the interview. Some companies deal only with certain recruiters, and individual résumés are often rejected. However, my master's degree from the Interdenominational Theological Center of the Atlanta University Complex, and the fact that I was currently teaching there may have prejudiced the individual to whom résumés were being sent. It was certainly no secret to anyone familiar with Atlanta that all of the schools in the Atlanta University Complex were, and still are, predominantly black.

My first interview with the company, Management Science America, Inc., was scheduled for a Saturday. This accommodated me perfectly as I taught no classes on the weekend or Monday. I did not expect the interview to last all day, but it did. There were several other applicants, for the company was rebuilding its technical staff, and each applicant had to be interviewed by multiple employees. At the end of the day, the interviewers asked a few of the applicants to come back on Monday to meet the executives. I was among the chosen few.

When I arrived on Monday, I was greeted by some of those with whom I had interviewed previously. They were somewhat apprehensive about my pending interview with the Boss. I was told to try not to be frightened or intimidated by the Boss's size. I was also informed that there had been no black professionals hired by the company and to expect some difficult questions. None of this was news to me; I always expected difficult questions. It had been my past experience that usually upon seeing me, interviewers seemed to feel the need to uncover my incompetence. So I told those who were concerned to relax. I was sure that I would be fine.

After having heard all about me from those who had previously interviewed me, I could only speculate as to why the Boss felt that I deserved special treatment. Perhaps he did not feel that he was competent to handle the interview alone, or perhaps he felt that I would be more intimidated by two white male executives. At any rate, he had asked one of his key managers from the New Jersey office to join him in my interview. Both men greeted me and asked me to be seated. I was asked some rather routine and expected questions, and I had the distinct feeling that the way I was responding was much more important than what I was saying.

The New Jersey manager never took his eyes off me while I responded to the satisfaction of the Boss, the obvious decision maker. Then the Boss turned the questioning over to his New Jersey manager, who observed me for what seemed to be a long time—but was probably no more than 30 seconds—and said, "I am not from the South, so I feel free to ask you anything I want to." I responded, "Please do." I knew that what he meant was that white Southerners were afraid to ask questions about race and he was not. He continued, "How has your being black helped or hurt your career?" I recognized this as a question designed to bring out the negatives of racism and the bitterness that many blacks feel. So I stared at him for a few seconds and boldly answered, "My being black has had no impact upon my career, for I have been eminently well qualified for every position I have ever had." He smiled and said, "I have no further questions."

The Boss then told me that he would let me know. I asked him, "When? I have another job offer." He responded, "Can you start next week?" I said, "Yes, but I am teaching graduate school and will only be able to work part-time for the next two months." He said, "No problem."

I asked him what the salary was, and he dismissed the New Jersey manager. He responded to my question by asking me how much I wanted. When I told him, he reduced the amount by $1,500 per year and said that I would get the rest in bonuses that were distributed every six months. I asked him how the bonuses were determined. He told me that they were his decision and based on merit. He said, "I am in a position to guarantee you at least $1,500 in bonuses your first year so that you will make the money you are asking for. This is my ball game, and I have the ball!" He also should have added, "And I make up the rules as we play."

Then he took me on a tour of the offices, introduced me as the newest employee, and told me that I would be receiving an official letter of offer in the mail. I tried to tell him what hours I would be available, but he told me to let my supervisor know. He added that whatever I could manage would be fine until I had fulfilled my teaching contract.

I was not given an official title, as most employees were simply classified as either technical or administrative. This lack of a title did not bother me initially, for the company was very loosely organized, and one could really assume any title he or she wanted. But in later years as the company became more formally organized, titles and the previous lack thereof became a disturbing factor.

From March until May 1973 I worked two part-time jobs, working for MSA all day on Monday and afternoons on Tuesday through Friday and then teaching Tuesday through Friday mornings. This initial part-time schedule was reminiscent of my early days at Burroughs when I was working and attending school. This time I was working and teaching school. Not only was I the first black technical employee (as had been the case at Burroughs, there was also a black man in the mailroom), but I was also the only part-time professional. Again, I learned to endure the stares and tried to master my new job.

In May I completed my teaching assignment, participated in the commencement exercises, and started working full-time as a part of the technical staff. This was the midpoint of my data processing career, for at this time I had worked for fourteen years. Little did I know that I would work in a corporate setting for only fourteen more years and that I would spend them all at MSA.

8

Returning to the Corporate South

$\mathcal{M}$y return to corporate America in the South rekindled the exposure to racism that had lain dormant during my tenure at the Interdenominational Theological Center. My first assignment with MSA was to write a sales brochure for the payroll accounting system. This assignment afforded me with the opportunity to learn the payroll system while using the literary talents acquired through the years of writing and teaching while living in Chicago. Needless to say, I was very excited about successfully completing this task.

I invested all of my energies in attempting to do the best job possible in record time. After all, this was my first assignment and, as usual, I wanted to prove that I was exceptional. I wrote as fast as I could and accordingly wanted the material typed in record time so that I could proof it and rewrite it. Soon the first problem arose.

The secretary assigned to type my work was white, and she not only resented having to type for me, but she also felt that I wanted my work returned in an unreasonably short period of time. As had many with whom I had worked before her, she stared at me, gave me evil looks, and would not speak unless forced into it by my persistence. She started putting other work ahead of mine, knowing that I had an important deadline to meet. The payroll brochure should have been rewritten long before, and it was desperately needed as it was one of the best selling products the company offered. I am sure she knew that delaying my work would anger me, and being angered, I just might cause a scene or in some other way behave unprofessionally—thereby proving that I was unworthy of the position for which I had been hired.

I do not know whether she had ever been exposed to a black professional before, but I am confident that she did not expect me to respond the way I did. I simply could not sit around while she sabotaged my Herculean effort. I immediately went to the Boss, bypassing my manager, and told him what was happening. He said that she was either to type my work as top priority with expediency or she could be replaced. He further commented, "I can bring secretaries in here by the truck load, but individuals like yourself who can and will write my brochures are few and far between. Let me know if you have any more trouble."

The secretary was not overjoyed with my report of the Boss's comments, but she did begin to type my work. However, she was unnecessarily sloppy, resentful, and slow. When I confronted her concerning the quality of her work, she came close to telling me how she felt about having to work for me; but noting the look in my eyes, she hesitated, thought about it, and refrained. I always had the feeling that she wanted to tell me something, and in all probability her hesitancy lay in the fact that she did not know how I would respond. Many white people are afraid of blacks and are reluctant to spark the militancy that they are certain lies dormant within even the most cultured or refined black. On the other hand, she did not know that I would not have lowered myself to fight or even argue with her, but I did expect my work to be completed with speed and accuracy.

She finally tired of both my pointing out her errors and my

resubmitting her work for corrections, and she quit. Because the office staff was so small, the friction between us was no secret. Although everyone in the office knew that racism was the cause of the friction, no one publicly admitted it or even acknowledged that there was a problem. It was just casually suggested that it would be wise to have me interview the next secretary, thereby letting her know in advance that she would be working for a black woman who expected top quality performance. I know that these concessions were made because no one else wanted to write the sales brochure. The Boss, for whom I was really working, even though I had another manager, was very hard to please, and he seemed satisfied with my work. Again I was noting that work that contributes to bottom-line profits is valued, and the color of the contributor is forgiven.

Although I was not authorized to hire, I could reject applicants. After interviewing two or three secretaries, a very competent young woman was hired with my approval. She admitted that she had never known a black professional before, and she was fascinated by me. She made every effort to please me, and most of her work was error-free.

My relationship with this young woman was the first of several similar ones I would develop with other white secretaries. I was for each a novelty, a new experience in supervisor-subordinate relationships. Each had to deal with me in her own way. Many were proud to have me become that one best, black friend about whom they could talk with their other friends to prove they were not prejudiced. During this period of Title VII legislation and Equal Employment Opportunity, it was beneficial—even fashionable in selected settings—to be liberal.

Because most of my secretaries were very young—often just out of high school—and I was a mother, I often became an advisor with regard to their personal affairs. My being a minister's wife also provided an air of professionalism to any advice I might offer. And then, one must remember that the Southern tradition placed the black "mammy" in the role of mother, advisor, and confidante to its Southern belles. I did not object to this role, for it was one with which they could live. It gave them comfort, and I had accepted the fact that I have a strong maternal instinct. I also believed that by actively witnessing to my faith, I could help some of them to become actively involved in the life of their church. I always invited my secretaries to my church and advised them to join and/or attend their own churches, read and study the Bible regularly, and to be constant in prayer. I believed and I told them that God would himself provide the answers to their problems; all they needed to do was trust him.

But for most of the men who were either my peers or my superiors, there was no comfortable role. I could not be a friend, a sex object, or a mother. And they just were not ready to accept me as an equal. Most of their wives were homemakers, and I was constantly asked, "How does your husband feel about your working?" They would observe that the majority of the other professional women in the office were single, and I not only had a husband, but also two small sons. I responded that my husband supported my working, helped me with the children, and knew that I needed to work for my own self-fulfillment. I also commented that the money helped us to live the kind of life we wanted. Judging by their responses, I know that if their wives had been able to contribute a salary like mine to their households, their quality of life would have improved. But I am sure that they were willing neither to have it appear that they could not adequately provide for their families nor to assist with the children and the household chores. White Southern pride was alive and well in my work environment.

The MSA payroll accounting system sales brochure was finished and extremely well received. The general feeling was that perhaps it had not been a mistake after all to have hired a black female. This consensus was reminiscent of the atmosphere after my first few successes with Burroughs Corporation. Co-workers who had hardly spoken to me prior to the printing of the brochure made it a point to tell me how they knew all along that I would do a super job. Encouragement before the completion of the project would have been much more welcome than was the praise afterwards.

My next assignment was to prepare minutes of the payroll system users' meeting in such a way that they could be published and distributed to all users. The speed with which I could write was directly responsible for my getting this assignment. But it was also true that none of the men wanted to sit in a meeting and take notes; and the general feeling among the executives was that the subject matter was much too complicated to be understood, recorded, and then interpreted for user distribution by a secretary. This was an extremely sexist attitude; yet no one saw it as such—just as no one chose to see the racist attitudes that surrounded us. I took the minutes, had them published, and distributed them to the users in less than a month. This had never happened before, and naturally it meant that recording the minutes would be my job for several years to come.

During that payroll meeting, a picture was taken of me and two white male peers sitting together. That picture appeared in the next annual report. The caption merely alluded to the number of data processing years the three of us collectively represented; however, the picture also revealed that for the first time in the history of the company, there was a black professional aboard. It was still fashionable in the early 1970s to demonstrate one's sense of fairness by hiring at least one token black. Although the Boss had admitted that he was not interested in tokenism and had said that he would not hire anyone—black or white—unless he or she was qualified, he was happy to have one black to display in his annual report!

After I became firmly entrenched in the payroll system, my next assignment was to write or direct the writing of a payroll users manual, a how-to book. My prior experience in writing programmed instruction textbooks was considered to be valuable in this effort. The Boss and I met to assign specific employees to each chapter. I was to write the first three chapters and allow them to be the format for all the others. Then I was to edit the work submitted by all other employees.

This was not a welcome task, for many of our technicians had neither skill nor interest in writing, and claimed that they had no time. I not only had to plead and beg, but also often had to do the writing myself in order to complete the assignment on time. Of course, no one cared whether my assignment was completed on time, for they knew that I, not they, would be held accountable. Being accustomed to working against all odds, I completed the work and the manual became a prototype for all other MSA systems.

I had proven myself. I had successfully completed all initial assignments. I was generally accepted for my competency, if not for my race, and I was rewarded. I did get those bonuses that I had been promised, and I did make more that first year than I had asked for during the hiring process. I felt that I was now ready for upward mobility, and it started to come in a way I had not expected—exposing me to a corporate America I did not know existed.

9

Upward Mobility

❧

*W*hen one works for a marketing company, the only way upward mobility can be expected is through visible proof that one's efforts have resulted in tangible sales. In other words, one must be able to demonstrate a positive contribution to the bottom-line sales figures. Writing sales brochures, documentation, and user meeting minutes—although indirectly responsible for increased sales—did not help me obtain the mobility I had envisioned.

So I sought the marketing path and asked to be more directly involved with the customer. After my prior exposure to Southern racism while working for Burroughs Corporation, I do not know why I did not stop to consider that there might still be some people who would not appreciate a black woman's coming into their firm to offer software solutions. But I am sure that the Boss did consider it. Rather than offer me a position as a technical presales consultant, he asked me to work on the design of a new Human Resource System that would incorporate some of the governmentally required Equal Employment Opportunity and Affirmative Action Reports.

Many black managers of the 1970s were involved in EEO and AA affairs. They would probably still be primarily concentrated in these areas if it were not for the fact that in the 1980s no one was very interested in EEO and AA. The Reagan administration, along with its realignment of the United States Supreme Court, changed that emphasis. Consequently, in the 1990s it is also true that no one is very interested in having black managers as their token concession to EEO and AA requirements.

Once I had developed a tentative system design, I was to visit several customers to find out whether the design on which I was working would actually satisfy their needs. Such movement would give me an opportunity to meet customers and to learn, through its development, a new system, which I could in turn help to market. I accepted this assignment willingly and soon had a design that I was ready to test on some customers who had been personally selected by the Boss. I am sure that the Boss's selections were based on location (away from the South), and his perception of their willingness to work with a black female consultant.

I was told that most of these customers who were interested in participating in the design phase were located in the Northeast, and my first visit was to be to Boston. This time I did think about the fact that the Southern customers might not have been willing to cooperate with me. However, I did not allow this to shake my confidence; I simply considered this to be their loss, and prepared for the Boston trip.

Having traveled all over the United States on business, I was not prepared for my Boss's suggestion that I stop at our New Jersey office where I would be met by one of our technical presales consultants who would accompany me to Boston. I did not understand why I needed an escort, but I am sure that it was the Boss's way of playing the 'Great White Father' and protecting an innocent black girl from ultimate disaster. It was also probably his way of traveling to the places I was to go in advance of my visit in much the same way my Burroughs manager had done. Both were very aware of the racist attitudes I would face, but while my former boss was willing to admit them, my current Boss was not. My current Boss had been born and raised in the South, and sending a companion with me was his way of protecting me while preserving his Southern pride. It would have been too painful for him to admit that he knew that racism was alive and well. He also knew that he would have exhibited the same racist attitude toward me if he were the client and I were coming to interview him. But, again, I had proven myself to be different—that special black exception who should be protected from the harsh realities of the real world.

I did not make it easy for him. I explained that I did not need an escort, and he was forced to provide me with a logical reason for his suggestion. I was told that this particular consultant knew the client, would introduce me, and would assist in noting any design changes that were required. Recalling that I was still relatively new to the company and that we were embarking on a major system design, I conceded that perhaps I was being sensitive with regard to the additional consultant's accompanying me on the trip. At any rate, I knew that resisting his suggestion would be to no avail. He was the Boss and he had decided.

I flew to New York, visited the New Jersey office, and continued to Boston with my fellow consultant, who happened to be a white male. As we checked into the hotel, racism reared its ugly head. When the hotel desk clerk saw us, he asked, "One room or two?" We responded, "Two." Then the clerk said, "How many in each room?" By this time, I was becoming perturbed, so my companion answered, "One." The clerk looked at us suspiciously, wondering why we were together if we were not really together.

We retired to our rooms and decided to meet later for dinner. Knowing that Boston was famous for its seafood, we went to a popular seafood restaurant. The restaurant was crowded and we had to wait for a table. While we were waiting, I noticed that many people were staring at us.

We were engaged in pleasant conversation when an elderly white woman interrupted us. She said, "You two look so happy. Have you been married long?" I was too shocked by her assumption to respond, but my companion responded, "Not long." Then the woman continued, "Do you have any children?" He answered "Three." (He was counting my two and his one.) The woman said, "That's so nice." And she walked away, but continued to stare.

The thought that the two of us could have been business associates never occurred to either the desk clerk or the elderly woman. The clerk, probably because he was at a hotel, assumed we were there for some sort of sexual liaison, and the woman, seeing us at a nice restaurant and neatly attired, assumed we were married. The racism that was inherent in each of their thought processes did not accommodate a business relationship between a white man and a black woman.

The people back in our respective offices thought that this little episode was funny, and from that point on my companion was known as my "on the road husband." My real husband called my attention to the racist attitudes expressed by the hotel clerk and the elderly woman that had made me so uncomfortable both during and after the trip; my companion's wife asked what we were doing that made the woman think we looked so happy.

As a result of the discussions and the teasing regarding my relationship to the New Jersey consultant, the Boss decided that perhaps it would be better if I continued my system design fact-finding trips alone. After all, as I am sure he reasoned, we could not have anyone thinking that our company actually encouraged relationships between white men and black women—at least not in a business environment. I also think that he had decided that I could handle the racist attitudes alone.

One subsequent trip to a client in Milwaukee was especially memorable. As had been the case when I worked for Burroughs at Georgia Tech, I had made all of the arrangements prior to the visit via the telephone. Again, it was believed by the client that I was the secretary of the man—the white man—who would be making the visit. This was perfectly logical, for not many women, and surely not a black woman, could know enough about the design of a human resource system to ask the proper questions. So, when I arrived in Milwaukee, I was greeted with a shocked expression. "Are you really Marjorie Kimbrough, the one who is supposed to ask the questions regarding system design?" I smiled and said, "Yes, I am." Then the disoriented response: "Well, we spoke with Marjorie, and . . . and we did not know that was you, and . . . and we really thought she was setting up an appointment for her boss." How much more of a dead giveaway would you want? Once the client recovered from the shock of my physical being, we actually accomplished the work for which I had come. I pretended that I did not notice the uneasiness, assumed my most professional attitude, and proceeded with the questions I had outlined. The session was a success, marked with intelligent responses.

Upon my return from that trip, I was told that perhaps I should carry a scrub brush in my briefcase. Then, whenever I was greeted in that same way, I could take out the scrub brush and say, "Oh, do you think this would be more appropriate as a tool of my trade?" Everyone laughed, but they were all aware that I was confronting very real racism in the 1970s in both the North and the South!

But I was moving up, and I had been noticed by others making the upward climb. That same New Jersey manager who had participated in my final interview with the Boss was one of three managers promoted to product development vice president. After his promotion had been announced, he drew me aside and asked me to be his assistant, really his "Girl Friday." He was the only one of the three promoted who was not located in the Atlanta corporate headquarters. Although he was scheduled to be transferred, he knew that he would need someone to be his Atlanta eyes and ears until that transfer could be effected.

Being extremely naive to the competitiveness of the small business environment, I did not understand what he wanted me to do. He explained that each of the three vice presidents would be in fierce competition with the others and that one of them would eventually be managing the other two. Someone would have to watch everything the other two were doing and report to him so that he would be well aware of their moves during his period of relocation. I asked, "Why me?" He responded, "I have watched you, and I don't believe that you would stab me in the back. And, if you do, then I deserve it for having so misread you."

Up until that time, I had thought that we were all on the same team. But we were actually on three separate teams. Only one would win. The New Jersey manager's product assignment was the human resource area, and that was the one in which I had established the most expertise. So I was on his team. I agreed to be his Atlanta contact, and he became both my manager and my mentor.

Although I did not know it at that time, in a small company, once one has made an alignment with an upwardly mobile mentor, no other alignment is possible. No other manager or potential mentor will ever trust you. If your mentor wins the much sought after promotion, you will be rewarded. If he does not win, neither will you. Within each company there is a real war being fought, and there are genuine masters of the game. Every player must be willing to pull out all of the stops. They must watch and analyze every move that is made. They must arrive early and stay late. I was not prepared to participate in this battle, but I was learning.

The three managers who were promoted at the same time

were not just managing the development of their products, they were also managing its marketing. They directed the development of its technical presentation, determined (along with client input) product enhancements, and assisted in product presentations and training. This, of course, is a lot of work, but it is also routine in small companies. Each manager selected key people to help direct these areas, and each sought to do a better job than was being done by the others.

I was already assisting my manager in product design and enhancement, but I was asked to help develop a new technical presentation and to plan some training for both customers and internal employees. Again, I jumped at the chance to do these jobs, seeing them as an opportunity to help my manager—and in turn myself—win in his struggle to reach the top.

Because my manager was especially good at making presentations on the existing product, I developed a new presentation on the product that I was helping to design. I designed visuals and trained other consultants to make that presentation. I traveled all over the nation to assist sales representatives, and resulting sales were fantastic. I was finally, visibly contributing to bottom-line profits.

My manager was pleased, but the Boss viewed me as the authority on the new product, not the old one. He felt that we should add a Southern Gentlemen to our team who could acquire experience with both the old and the new systems. The Boss still did not believe that I could be used effectively in sales in the South, so he labeled the new employee the Southern counterpart to my manager. Well, immediately I knew that I would have problems with the Southern Gentleman.

I really do not know what it is, but sometimes I can see prejudice written all over certain faces. This man had one of those faces, and we were jointly assigned to work on a task. Because I had been with the company longer and knew the assignment, I assumed some leadership for it. This was a

mistake as far as he was concerned, for as a Southern
Gentleman, he was certainly not accustomed to working jointly
with a black woman—especially one who had the audacity to
take control.

We had our first words when he ignored everything I did and
began to give me orders. I let him know that we were working
together; I was not working for him. He intimated that he had
been assigned to the project because I could not handle it alone.

One of the first things a white man tries to do is to undermine
the black man's or woman's confidence. If he could convince
me that I was not capable of doing the job alone, then he would
be in control. Of course, this did not work with me. I had had
too many successes, and I knew that if anyone could do the job,
I could.

I accused him of being both racist and sexist, and told him
that I would not put up with either. He pretended to be shocked
and explained that never in his life had he been so accused. He
went on to tell me that his secretary at his former job had been
black, and they had had a very close relationship. I told him that
that was probably because she did work for him, and he had
probably treated her like a servant. In his mind such treatment
would have been appropriate for a secretary, especially a black
one. He then told me that the only reason I was so uppity with
him was that both the Boss and the manager liked me and that
when he got to be the boss, I would not be number one anymore.
I responded by saying that when he got to be the boss, I would
not be around anymore.

My manager did not like the fact that two of his best people
were bickering, and he asked us to call a truce. He also tried,
from that point on, to keep us working on separate projects. But
I had the last word when I was asked to purchase gag gifts for
members of our product team. These gifts were to be
representative of things with which each of us had become
associated. For example, one of our consultants who never

remembered to call the office when she was on the road was given a toy telephone. I was given that scrub brush symbolic of perceived subservience to carry in my briefcase. But I gave the Southern Gentleman a white sheet, symbolic of the Ku Klux Klan. We all laughed at our gifts, but he was disturbed by his. He complained to me that others might really believe him to be prejudiced. I told him that he really was.

This Southern Gentleman distanced himself from me and from the managers who supported me by accepting, perhaps even requesting, a transfer to an office in a city where he had the opportunity to manage. He had decided that his climb upward would fare better away from the manager he sought to replace. He was right in this assessment. Both married and single men seeking the upward climb often decide to relocate.

Although single woman may, married women usually do not. When you are playing the game to win, you must weigh all of your options. The loyalty I had to my husband and to my manager kept the possibility of relocation from ever entering my mind. And even if I had considered it, there would not have been a management position available for me. There were still no other black professionals employed by the company in any location, and no women in significant management.

Part of my strategy for upward mobility was to become the best at presenting my product. I was generally considered to be the best, and frequent requests for my assistance in product presentations came from sales representatives in the North, East, and West. Very few came from the South. The reasons for this were several: salesmen did not want to travel in the South with a black woman; they were not sure about hotel accommodations, and no one wanted to be embarrassed. And most Southern companies were run by "good old boys" who just would not believe a black woman could tell them anything about software. There was also the consideration that part of my expertise was centered around the Equal Employment Opportunity and

Affirmative Action reporting capabilities available in the system, and the good old boys certainly did not want to be reminded of the need for that. So the Boss actually was right in his assessment of my Southern effectiveness. He was a Southerner, and he knew the South.

So a young, attractive, white Southern woman was hired as my assistant. She was instructed to learn everything I knew. She followed me around with a tape recorder, and she practiced making my presentations. I worked hard to help her become successful, for I felt that her success would continue to prove my worth. I knew there was nothing I could do to change some of the racist attitudes that I had encountered in both the North and the South, and if she was successful after having been trained by me, then I was successful. I even assisted her in the design of a new component of the system in compliance with employee benefits legislation that recently had been passed.

She was a good student, but like the Southern Gentleman, she assessed her possibilities for advancement in the same office with me and requested a transfer to a different one. She knew that she could be a star in another office, but she would always be my student as long as she was associated with me. She was single and very ambitious. There was not much that she was not willing to do to succeed. And on her way up, she did most of it.

After she was transferred, the development of that new benefits component was passed on to another new employee. He, like the Southern Gentleman and all of the top-level executives, was a white male Georgia Tech graduate—in fact a former star quarterback. I was assigned to train him, also. I helped him learn the system and made sure that the component being developed was in compliance with federal legislation. Afterward, he also transferred to another office for further advancement. This football player, the Southern Gentleman, and the attractive young woman would all reappear in my future corporate climb.

During this struggle up the corporate ladder, my family and I did have the satisfaction of being invited to socialize with my manager and his family in their home, and they, in turn, came to mine. Because this manager was also my mentor, he confided that he had mentioned to the Boss that I probably thought it strange not to be invited to socialize with him. He said that the Boss admitted not ever having thought of me in a social setting. His Southern upbringing did not allow interracial socialization. But, not wanting to hurt my feelings, the Boss did invite my family to his home. Both he and his boss (the top executive) and their families visited and ate in my home on several occasions. I never forgot my husband's warning that in their eyes I was still a "nigger," but I did feel that I was being accepted into the company and into their lives.

Whenever I had lunch with my mentor and other male colleagues at nearby Atlanta restaurants, I would be the object of numerous stares and glances. My mentor commented that in New York no one would even notice our being together, but I had to remember that Atlanta—while often referred to as "little New York"—was still in the South.

Often, well-meaning but prejudiced white women would approach our table and ask me, "Are you Diahann Carroll?" The question always shocked me because I really do not look like Diahann Carroll, but then I realized that the women asking were sure that I had to be some celebrity. What average black woman would be dining with several attractive white business men? This thinking was just another expression of their prejudice.

I continued to travel all over the nation making presales presentations and helping to close sales. This traveling caused some major adjustments at home. Determined to be "Super Mom," I cooked all day on Saturday preparing meals for the next week. Then I labeled the meals for each day, placed them in the freezer, and instructed my husband to take them out and put them in the oven or, in later years, the microwave so that there would be a home-cooked meal in case I was on the road.

I even got the boys' clothes together for each day, matching shirts, pants, and socks. I had discovered long ago that men really do not care what you do (within reason) as long as they are not inconvenienced. The first time they run out of clean underwear or home-cooked food, they decide that you care more about your career than you do about your family. It is at that point that the problems begin. I avoided that by working extra hard on the weekends preparing for the late work and travel possibilities of the coming week. Sometimes that preparation included lining up baby sitters for the evenings my husband had meetings at the church that he needed to attend. I know some people would say I did too much, but I felt better about leaving my family if I had provided for them. I could not have succeeded in any of it if my husband had not been supportive, but he was. And it worked.

While I was making my upward climb, my husband was making his. For the second time in his career, he was appointed as the first black pastor of a church in racial transition. Considerable hostility surrounded this appointment, for the white pastor who had preceded him did not want to be moved. So he conveniently forgot to leave the keys to the pastor's study, making it necessary to remove the door from its hinges in order to enter that first Sunday. Now this time I am talking about white Southern Christians, not corporate executives. Racism is everywhere, even in the church.

I knew that we would encounter both fear and hostility as we entered the new church, and I used the situation as an opportunity for office evangelism. I explained my husband's appointment to my co-workers and invited them to attend church on our first Sunday. Many of them, from top-level management to the mailroom clerk, did attend. As my manager said later, anyone who did not come almost admitted to being racist. Memories of our wedding came to mind. Whether they came because they did not want me to consider them racist, or whether they came to support me and my husband, I do not know. I do know that I appreciated their presence and that all the white members who had thought we were militant blacks were glad to discover that we knew white people who were not afraid of us.

Upward mobility for both me and my husband had begun, but as I continued my climb, I came face to face with corporate corruption.

10

Corruption Abounds

C orruption in corporate America assumes many forms. It may manifest itself as the unyielding quest for power. It may become the insatiable desire for sex. It may be realized as the never-ending need for money. It may evolve as the addiction to alcohol and drugs. It may manifest itself in racial and sexual prejudice. Or it may be evidenced in the abuse of subordinate employees. During my corporate encounter, I saw corruption in all of these forms, but I personally experienced racial and sexual prejudice. The amazing thing to me was that everyone else also saw the corruption that surrounded us, for there was certainly no attempt to hide it. We all discussed it, but no one ever did anything about it. I even discussed it with management, but either I was told that it was not proper for management to discuss that particular form of corruption with me, or the entire issue was simply acknowledged and ignored. The general thinking appeared to be that if the corruption was ignored long enough, it would eventually go away. I suppose management felt that trying to deal with corruption in any of its forms would require resources that were just not available. So, being unhampered, corruption flourished in all of its forms.

With each of the three newly appointed vice presidents firmly rooted in his own product area, the corrupting quest for power and control began in earnest. Each of the three assessed the strengths and weaknesses of the other two. Each sought to discover the particular form of corruption that could be used to defeat the other two. Each continued to assemble his individual supporting teams.

It soon became evident that one of these three was clearly the weakest. The vice president for whom I worked decided to ignore this weak vice president knowing that in time he would eliminate himself. But the other vice president decided to help push this weak man toward elimination. He started reopening and eventually winning accounts on which the weak man had given up, and he started casually mentioning, in appropriate places, both the weak man's poor appearance and lack of creative ideas. The Boss began to notice. Appearance is extremely important when one is playing the corporate game. If one expects to win, to reach the top, he must look the part. In comparison to the other two, the weaker vice president's appearance was poor. His suits were often dirty and his shirts were frayed.

The weak man happened to have a strong wife, and when one is fighting dirty, wives are included. Comments were circulated about how his wife had given up her job to accommodate her husband's corporate climb, and the general consensus was that this really should not have happened as she actually was the stronger of the two.

Gossip and rumors are a form of corruption, too. Managers talk to secretaries, and conversations are overhead in the bathroom, in elevators, in stairwells, and soon one's reputation is damaged. Someone from one of the opposing teams was always listening for bits of information that could be used against the other teams. A leader with a damaged reputation would certainly weaken the team.

Of course this weak vice president was no match for his opponent, and his actions tended to support the rumors that were being spread. Perhaps his supporting team should have counseled with him to help him improve his image and to avoid the obvious errors he was making in failing to follow through on prospective clients thought to be lost. But, being weak himself, he had surrounded himself with weak team players. Weak people select weak team players so that no team member will be able to outshine the leader. I would think that weak people would select strong people to help them, but no one ever believed that I really knew how to play the corporate game.

Before long that weak vice president had lost his area of product responsibility and was placed in a staff rather than a marketing position. Being removed from a position that could measurably contribute to bottom line profits is the kiss of death in a marketing company. With this action, everyone knew that he would no longer be featured in the annual report or mentioned among company leaders. Eventually even his title was taken from him, and finally he was forced to resign. Corporate promotions are as easily lost as won, and those who are not ready and willing to risk losing—whether through corruption or incompetence—should not play the corporate game at all.

So we were down to two viable candidates for control of all product development. The candidate who was not my manager correctly viewed me as a supportive team member of the opposing team. Though he probably could have used my talents, my solid alignment with his opponent prevented my being a member of his team. Even if he had been successful in having me transferred to his team, I am sure he believed that he would not be able to trust my loyalty to him. The only option was to have me removed from the opposing team.

Since I had proved myself to be a valuable employee and the top executives liked me, getting me fired was out of the question. The logical thing to do was to place me in neutral territory. Of course, all of this is only my opinion, but this is what I believe happened.

That opposing vice president began to talk to the Boss about the need for more sophisticated advertising. Up to this point, most of the advertising had been of the home-grown, cut and paste variety. But we were a growing company that could use a professional advertising agency. There was one problem; the Boss did not believe that there was an agency in Atlanta or anywhere else for that matter that knew enough about the software business to do a professional job of representing our company. I was suggested as a liaison. I knew the software business, I had some writing expertise, and whenever someone was needed for a job for which no one was known to be qualified, I was nominated. If I failed, it was because I was incompetent; if I succeeded, it was because I was that one exceptional black employee who had proven her worth many times over.

The opposing vice president had found the perfect way of removing me from my manager's side. I would be working for the Boss, and surely I would view that as a promotion. I became suspicious of the suggestion when the Boss spoke to me about the move before he spoke to my manager. I knew that he was the Boss, but there were some rules that even he did not usually violate. He approached me by saying that there comes a time when every ''plant needs to be repotted.'' He said that I needed a new challenge, and advertising and sales promotion would certainly provide that. He further reasoned that I had even had some experience in sales promotion by writing the sales brochure.

I explained that I had no advertising expertise and that I was happy doing the job I had as assistant to the vice president. He ignored my comment and continued by telling me that the agency could provide the advertising expertise, but I could provide the company expertise. He said, ''You are smart, and smart people can learn to do anything.'' He told me that I would be manager of creative services with my own staff. Although I was managing the clerical staff of my department, I did not really have my own staff. I asked for time to think about it. When I discussed the offer with my manager (mentor), he was angry because he had not been approached first. I believe he knew that my name had been suggested by his opponent. My manager suspected that the opposing vice president was trying to weaken him by removing one of his strongest team players, yet he could not resist having respect for the strategy that was being used against him. He also told me that the vice president who had been demoted had wanted this new advertising liaison job, and I would constantly have to watch my back. Everything I did would be criticized, and every attempt would be made to make me appear incompetent. But he promised to help me and said that my enemies would have to come through him to get to me. I believed him without considering the fact that when you are no longer on the same team, you are soon forgotten.

Nevertheless, he told me that he thought I should take the job. It was a good opportunity for me to work with the top company executives, and they were in a position to do much more for me than he could. I respected his advice, but I was reluctant to accept it because I was enjoying my work, and I felt protected being a part of his team. I also felt that his having come from a poor immigrant background helped him to understand my minority status in a company of white Anglo-Saxon males. None of the other executives shared this background.

I discussed the new position with my husband, who agreed that it was a move to place me in neutral territory, but I either had to accept it or quit. He said, ''You can't tell the Boss no.'' He also thought that I could help my manager by letting him know what was happening at the top. Then I realized that I could push for ads that would promote his product area, thus helping to boost his sales. I really did not want to leave the company, and I was grateful to my manager and felt that I could help him by taking the job.

Reluctantly, I took the job. This was the first time that I had accepted a job that I was not happy about. I think I knew that it would eventually lead to the end of my upward mobility with MSA, but at the time, I did not think I had any options.

My office was moved to the top floor near the Boss. The position of my office became key, for I could see who went in and out of the Boss's office. Sometimes one's physical presence can influence the Boss's decisions. The opposing vice president made many more trips to the Boss's office than my former manager did. I knew almost immediately that my mentor was losing, and if he was losing, so was I. But I also knew that part of the reason my mentor was losing was that I was no longer on his team.

Before long, the opposing vice president was made head of all development, and my former manager was reporting to him. Realizing that the game had been lost, some people would simply accept the loss and continue to work in whatever capacity they were given. But I knew that as soon as he had found another job, my mentor would quit. As he said to me, "When someone on an equal level with you is promoted over you, it is the same as saying that that person is better than you. No one is better than I am!" As I expected, he quit.

The new vice president in charge of all development then had the responsibility of finding a replacement for my former manager. He transferred the Southern Gentleman back and appointed him. For the first time, I was glad that I was no longer working on the human resource system. I decided to keep my distance.

I was having some successes with the creative services department, but it was difficult to please all of top management. Their preferred advertising styles were so different. Both the ad agency and I were frustrated, but we managed to produce some good sales promotion literature and some successful ads.

At times the Boss and I were at odds with each other. He would ask me to write something for him to submit to the ad agency. I would write it and he would say, "I don't like it. Do it again." I would ask "What don't you like? Give me some direction." He would reply, "I don't know. Just do it again. I'll know what I want when I see it." I tried to make him understand that different was not necessarily better. I sincerely believe he thought it was.

Sometimes I even made decisions without having received his final approval. When he discovered what I had done, he would be angry with me and would tell me that my action would cost the company money. One time I became so frustrated by his assumption of infallibility that I responded, "You are not God, and you are wrong!" He did not speak to me except when absolutely necessary for several weeks; but when my unapproved action resulted in positive benefits to the company, he simply called me and told me that he had new pictures of his children that he wanted me to see. This meant that I was forgiven and we could be friends again. He never apologized.

So, at this point in my career, I was meeting with the executive committee, working for the Boss, and helping to make important decisions—or at least I thought I was. It was during the production of an annual report that I found out differently.

Pictures were being taken of all members of the executive committee for the annual report. My picture was taken, but when the layout for the annual report featured my picture with the pictures of the other executives, the Boss was very disturbed. He let me know that my picture was to be included, but not with the executives. He said that just because I was included in the executive committee meetings did not mean that I was an executive. I was simply invited as his guest. I helped him remember things. In fact, he made it sound as though I was his secretary. Now at this time I was making $45,000 plus bonuses, or about $50,000 a year. White males whom I had trained were making about twice that amount.

I was hurt, nearly in tears, and remembering that I was a black woman, I thought, "How could I have elevated myself to the position of executive in a company run by white male Georgia Tech graduates?" I told the ad agency to take out my picture altogether.

The Boss, then feeling that his special relationship to me had been destroyed, told me that I would no longer be reporting to him but to the vice president who had outlasted both the weak vice president and my mentor, and had brought the Southern Gentleman back on the scene. I knew this was the kiss of death, but I tried to survive. I considered quitting, but by this time I had come to believe that all corporations were the same. I would simply have to prove myself all over again at a new company; I would have to discover who the snakes were and in which departments they were hiding; I would have to make new friends. By this time, I had decided that I was not playing the corporate game. I had been with this company for eight years; as long as they paid me my money, I would do my job.

I had only just begun working for my new manager when he announced that the Southern Gentleman wanted me back in the human resources area working for him. There were two factors working here. One, my new manager did not trust me because I had been closely aligned with his opponent. Two, the Southern Gentleman wanted to show me that he had finally won our old battle and had become the boss. Of course I did not want the assignment. But as my new manager put it to me, "You will either have to go to work for him, or he will see to it that you are fired because he knows that you know more about the human resource system than he does." Welcome to the real world, Margie!

My return to the human resource area was brief, for the first thing the Southern Gentleman did was cut my semi-annual bonus by $1,000. He said that he needed the money for some of the men who were supporting families and did not make as much money as I did. Considering my knowledge of EEO law, I was surprised that he would make such an admission to me, but he knew that I felt defeated and probably would not do anything about it. Then he started surrounding himself with his old friends. He recalled the Georgia Tech quarterback from the other office and announced that I would be reporting to him. Well, this was more than even I could bear, and I submitted my resignation.

I had trained that quarterback, and I knew more about the product than either he or the Southern Gentleman did. I was told that the quarterback was better known in the regional offices and would do a better job of managing the product marketing portion of the system. I laughed. I had been the first black professional hired by the company. I had developed the first system design and had given the initial presentations. Everyone knew me.

Upon receipt of my resignation, the Southern Gentleman asked me what he was doing wrong that was causing his good people like me to quit. I reminded him of the statement he had made when he was first hired. At that time he had said, "When I get to be the boss, you won't be number one anymore." My response had been that when he got to be the boss, I would not be around. I was simply fulfilling that promise by quitting. The quarterback, knowing I had been wronged, had tears in his eyes when he told me how sorry he was that I was leaving. And I am sure that he *was* sorry, for he was counting on me to do most of his work. The other people in the department encouraged me to file a discrimination suit, and I went to the Office of Equal Employment Opportunity. After talking with an EEO counselor, I was told that I had an excellent case, but I already knew that.

When the vice president of all development received my resignation, he asked to see me. With a smile on his face, he asked me why I was quitting. I told him that I had trained that football player and certainly had no intention of working for him. I was already knee deep in incompetence. The vice president tried to undermine my confidence, but I was ready for him. I told him that he was entitled to his opinion; in fact, I was accustomed to the prejudiced opinions of white men like him. For that very reason I had majored in mathematics in college. I explained to him that in math, answers are either right or wrong; they are never subject to prejudice or opinion. In like manner, I did not have to rely on his opinion either to assess my competence or to find me work. I knew who I was, and I was certainly more competent than anyone I was currently working for. He was distressed to discover that his particular brand of corruption—prejudice—was not working on me in the way he had anticipated. I am sure he knew that the Boss, though estranged from me, would contact me and would not want to lose me as an employee.

Our conversation ended in a shouting match, and I was so angry that I was in tears. During this argument, his secretary later told me that she had stayed near the door in order to make sure that I was all right. I went home determined to sue and to quit.

The top company executive called me at home and asked me to meet him in his office the next day. When I arrived, the Boss was there, too. They both apologized for the Southern Gentleman's insensitivity, but told me that they thought that the football player was the best choice for the job. They felt compelled to stand by the decision that had been made whether they really agreed with it or not. Good old boys do stick together. I told them that I did not understand their reasoning; I was better qualified on every score. I told them that I was not a white male Georgia Tech graduate, but that I would put my Phi

Beta Kappa key from the University of California next to their Georgia Tech degrees any day.

Now remember that prior to these demotions I had been reporting directly to the Boss, a white male Georgia Tech graduate who reported to the top executive, also a white male Georgia Tech graduate. After that I was reporting to the vice president, a white male Georgia Tech graduate who reported to the Boss. Next, I was reporting to the Southern Gentleman, a white male Georgia Tech graduate who reported to the vice president. Then I was to report to the football player, a white male Georgia Tech graduate who reported to the Southern Gentleman. I had started out one level away from the top level executive and had ended up four levels away with a string of white male Georgia Tech graduates in between.

Of course, no matter what I said, neither the top executive nor the Boss could go against the decision of their middle management, so they tried to offer me a compromise. The Boss announced that he had told the vice president with whom I had had the shouting match to stay away from me. Then they asked me what I wanted to do since I had refused to work for the football player. They did agree that my refusal was certainly understandable, even expected, in light of the fact that the Southern Gentleman had handled the situation so poorly. They said that he just did not understand women like me, meaning proud black women. I told them that I did not think that there was anything for me to do. Then the top executive asked me to write a job description of what I would like to do. He would review it, and if there was such a job, I could have it. If there was no such job, he would help me find a job at another company. I told them that if I remained, no future job could, in any way, report to the vice president, the Southern Gentleman, or the football player. They agreed.

Thus, having ruled out all of development, the only job possible for me had to be with marketing. I had to weigh my options. Did I really want to describe a marketing position that I could probably get, or did I want to proceed with my lawsuit? Knowing EEO law, and having already talked with a counselor, I definitely had a good case. I was a black female, over forty, with more seniority than the football player, who was a white male under forty. My record of presales presentations had resulted in more sales than his had; I had designed the system presentation and written the sales brochure; all of my performance and salary reviews had been favorable; and I had trained the football player. I was sure that I could win the lawsuit, but what good would it do me? The EEO case backlog was such that it would be months if not years before the case was heard. What would I do in the meantime? Even if I did win, would any other company in the industry risk hiring me? Did I even want the job for which I had been passed over if it meant working for the Southern Gentleman? I decided to drop the lawsuit and described a job as a human resource industry specialist working for industry marketing. This would place me on the marketing side of the company and would allow me to return to consulting, which I had always preferred. The job description I wrote was one for which I was uniquely qualified, and the top executives were pleased to transfer me to industry marketing. This allowed me to temporarily sidestep direct confrontation with corruption. Although I did not know it at the time, the stock that I would have had to relinquish had I resigned eventually came to be worth a considerable amount of money. So my decision to stay definitely proved to be a profitable one when the company went public a few years later.

11

Changes in Management

❦

$\mathcal{M}$anagement Science America, Inc., entered a period of rapid growth. There were acquisitions; European, Australian, and Asian expansions; and changes in management. I was working on the marketing side of the company, but I was attending industry meetings, giving presentations, and recommending marketing strategies to my new manager. I stayed away from the top executives, for I knew that I was not popular after having quit publicly, having my resignation returned, and then having been transferred to a new position. When such events occur, it appears as though management has made a mistake, and we all know that that never happens.

My new manager was a certified public accountant who had formerly worked for an MSA client. He had oversold his capabilities and had been hired to design a new accounting module for one of the systems. Having failed at this assignment, he was promoted to manager of the industry marketing group. His promotions continued to amaze me, for he, like so many others, kept failing and yet kept being promoted. But, as I would later discover, he had not yet risen to his highest level of incompetence.

My first real encounter with him came at the semiannual bonus distribution. The bonuses had always been a source of concern. I had spent most of the six-month bonus period in the Southern Gentleman's group, and I knew that he certainly had not allocated any bonus money for me. In fact, he had cut my bonus the last time. I had not been in the new group long enough to make a substantial contribution to sales, but I was eligible. If I was not to receive a bonus, someone would have to tell me why. I really do not think anyone wanted that assignment in light of what we had just been through.

So my manager took me to lunch and explained that although at first I had not been allotted a bonus, an amount had been made available because what had happened to me was as much management's fault as it was mine. I could not believe what I was hearing. This idiot was actually tell me that discrimination was partly my fault! He went on to tell me that he had no problems with race or sex. Immediately a flag lit up that said, "Thou dost protest too much!" It has never failed in my experience that when one boasts of his liberalism and his interracial friends, there is a streak of prejudice lurking in the background. But I had decided that I was not playing the corporate game, so I accepted the bonus check by simply saying, "Thank you." For once I managed to keep my mouth closed. It had simply become too stressful to fight.

Having discovered that I was again reporting to a manager who was both prejudiced and incompetent, I decided that I had better make myself as valuable as possible so that there would be no opportunity for my dismissal. I had certainly made some enemies, and they were not above trying to get me fired. Again I was assisting nationally in presales presentations, and I was involved in seeing that the changes and rulings with regard to federal law as they affected the human resource system were applied. I wrote memos to my manager documenting the ways in which the system was affected and copied the Southern Gentleman. I did not write to him directly as I was no longer involved in development.

Then my manager, failing to make the industry marketing group the kind of visible entity that had been envisioned, was promoted to company officer status. At this point he had reached the height of his incompetence, and soon he mysteriously left the company.

With this mysterious departure of its manager, the industry marketing group was viewed as one that would be difficult to successfully develop. Difficult tasks were always given to people, usually women or blacks, who were expected to fail. In the past, I had always been given difficult tasks, but in this particular case, the task was given to a white woman who had recently been named vice president. She was the first woman vice president of the company and, incidentally, she was seen as one who would probably fail no matter what task she was assigned. I am not sure whether she was promoted because there were no female officers or because her chances of succeeding were virtually nonexistent. Sometimes not having a female officer can be justified when the token who is finally appointed subsequently fails. It can then be said that it was known all along that no woman could succeed and that is the reason one had never been appointed.

This was my first experience with reporting to a woman, and she was well aware of the problems I had previously encountered. She even discussed some of the problems she had had in her upward climb. She said that, in contrast to me, she had decided to play the corporate game and that she had won the first battle: she had become an officer. I wished her well, but told her that I was not willing to sacrifice my family and my personhood to play the corporate game. At least, in her struggle, she did not have to overcome the color barrier. But she did have a problem with self-confidence. She even sought outside help to instill greater confidence and self-esteem. That outside assertiveness group eventually may have been her undoing.

In addition to the industry marketing group, she was also responsible for the corporate marketing group, which included advertising and public relations. This latter group was a new expanded version of the creative services group I had previously managed. Most of the work that had been purchased outside in the past was now being handled in-house. Some talented people had been hired, but the same old executive thinking was running the show. The woman vice president had her work cut out for her. She did not know that she would have to work closely both with the Boss, who had no respect for her, and with the top executive, who had sponsored her, and that they had very different ideas about the corporate image that needed to be projected.

Meanwhile there were other changes in management. A microcomputer software company was purchased, and there were some shifts in mainframe management to accommodate this acquisition. It appeared to me that any manager who was in trouble with mainframe development was sent to work on the micro side. Both the Southern Gentleman and the football player were sent to the micro side with the football player being transferred to an office in another state. This came as no surprise, because I knew that neither of them would succeed.

The attractive, young Southern woman who had been hired as my assistant had made some friends while working in a regional office, and she was transferred back to corporate headquarters in a management capacity. She was working on the development side of the company, but she wanted to be involved in marketing. She was no smarter than she had been when she worked for me, but she had become much more cunning. She was a true game player, and she eventually got what she wanted one way or another.

The woman vice president began to lose ground and people. Again it became evident that I was working for the losing side.

The vice president decided that he had better take control of the industry marketing group and incorporate it within the various development teams. Of course, after my prior confrontations, the woman knew that I would not work for any group that reported to the vice president, so she asked if I would like to work in the corporate marketing group. I asked what I would be doing. She said, "Oh, the same thing that you currently do." I said, "You mean that I will be the only industry marketing specialist who reports to corporate marketing?" She responded affirmatively and then added that I would be doing other things as well. Having lost all interest in the games that were being played, I simply agreed.

The part of corporate marketing to which I was transferred did have a manager. She was a Southern woman who did not have the vaguest notion of how to deal with me. I had more experience, more company and industry knowledge, more education, more everything. But I was well accustomed to less competent managers. She knew me to be an intelligent and outspoken person, and she decided to let me do whatever I wanted to.

My new group consisted entirely of women. This was a new experience for me. In all of my years, I had never worked in an all-female group. These women began to view me as a mother, leader, or advisor, and they soon came to me for all decisions—professional and personal. The manager came to me, too, and it was obvious to everyone that I was managing the group. The woman vice president may have had this in mind when she assigned me to the group, for she knew that the group's manager needed help. It always turned out that in a supporting role I somehow emerged as the leader although I was not recognized as such. Again I had been strategically placed to help a white manager who was incapable of helping himself or, in this case, herself.

I continued with my work as before and accepted a project of developing an effective presentations course to be taught to all employees involved in making presentations. The woman vice president told me that it was generally conceded by top executives that I gave the best presentations in the company and that surely there were some skills that I could teach others. Having minored in speech at the university, I found developing a syllabus on effective presentation skills both easy and enjoyable.

With the first overwhelmingly successful courses, the demand for my time in teaching could have easily been full-time. But I did not want to become a teacher. I wanted to be directly involved with the clients in marketing software. I divided my time as best I could and continued to act as my own manager. I volunteered to learn how to use the microcomputer and to give the micro-to-mainframe computer demonstrations at trade shows. At least in this way I kept client contact and felt that I was growing. During all of this time, I was ignored by the Boss and the top executive who had worked so hard to keep me from leaving the company. It is a real atrocity when one has to struggle to find his or her own ways of developing skills and growing when one works for a company that prides itself on caring about the employee and having as its motto, ''People Are the Key.'' Yes, people are the key as long as they are the right people from the right schools who are the right sex and the right color. I was none of the above, but somehow I was still valuable, or maybe my earlier threatened EEO suit was just intimidating.

My manager, who did not realize that she was not really managing her group, became increasingly disturbed by the woman vice president's lack of management skills and resigned. She confided in me that she felt the woman was losing ground rapidly and would soon lose all of her groups. She felt that it was in her best interest to move on. She was also, though she did not admit it, very much disturbed that she did not have control of her own group. I did.

With the departure of this manager, the woman vice president asked me to manage the group. I accepted even though the assumption of management status was meaningless. I did not begin to do anything that I had not already been doing, with the exception of signing the group's time and expense reports, and I did not make any more money. I did receive the confidential memos that were sent to management only, and my name was listed along with the other marketing managers.

I mention this only because shortly after I accepted this position, the woman vice president hired an advertising manager and then tried to deny my management status by making him my manager. He was a man who had considerable experience in both advertising and management, and he had no one to manage. I believe she told him that he could share my secretary until he hired his own and that my group and I would report to him. She just never told me any of this. So, when he started acting like my manager, we had problems. I started having visions of my first experiences with the Southern Gentleman's trying to manage me when we had the same management status.

I really do not know why the woman vice president never said anything to me about the new manager or my status in light of his position. Many have suggested that she was threatened by me or that she was even afraid of me and that it was easier for her simply to say nothing. She even did things like quietly forget my salary and performance reviews. Whenever I would mention them to her, she would say that she just had not gotten around to it. When I finally went over her head to her boss, he asked whether or not there was a problem between us. I told him that if there was, I just did not know what it was. I did eventually get my raises, but she never discussed them with me. I had to calculate the percentage increase as there was always retroactive pay included due to the fact that they were several months late. I never got a performance review. I am sure that she did not feel capable of giving me one.

There was definitely a strained relationship between us, and I distinctly noticed it when I approached her about the possibility of my husband's being transferred to New York.

A large congregation in New York was conducting a nation-wide search for a new pastor. My husband was one of those being considered. I informed the woman vice president and the top executives that my family was going to New York to be interviewed for the position. I felt that the Boss had had enough time to forgive me for quitting, and I wanted to see whether he would offer me a job with the company in New York. He did encourage me to talk with the New York office to consider the possibilities of transferring; and although he did not offer me a job in the New York office, the top company executive did guarantee me one if I moved.

My husband was offered the position; but after careful consideration, he declined the offer. This was the best decision for the family, but it did not seem to be the best decision for my career. It was best for the family because our older son was entering his senior year in high school, had just been elected student body president, and was academically at the top of his class. Of course, he did not want to move. I agreed that he should not have to move and had made arrangements with a neighbor for him to remain in Atlanta. Also, our younger son, having two remaining years of high school, would have had to attend a private school in order to get the same quality of education. The cost of the school was in excess of $5,000 a year. And the cost of living in New York was much greater than it was in Atlanta, yet there was to be no increase in family income. But perhaps most important of all was that my husband did not have a good feeling about the move. We strongly believe in divine guidance, and if the move did not feel like it was what God was leading him to do, I did not want him even to consider it.

At first I thought it probably was not the best decision for my career because I was offered a position as human resource consultant and education center manager in the New York office. This would have provided me with the presales opportunities I enjoyed, as well as management responsibilities in neutral territory, one in which I was respected. It would have also removed me from the woman vice president, who was obviously in trouble with the company and somewhat uncomfortable with me. In addition, my mentor, having previously returned to the New York area, heard about my possible move and called to offer me a position with his new company at a substantial increase in salary. But I had decided long ago that my husband would make those major career decisions for our family; and I believe that, although it did not appear so at the time, it ultimately was the best decision for my career, also. At any rate, I am satisfied that we did what God wanted us to do.

Meanwhile, back at the office, neither the new advertising manager nor the woman vice president ever said anything to me about a change in my reporting status. If one is never informed of changes in management and one's time and expense reports continue to be sent to and signed by the same person, there is no reason to believe that there has been a change. Such was the case with me and my group. None of us ever believed that we reported to the advertising manager.

The real problem occurred at the infamous bonus time. The advertising manager, without consulting me, decided on the bonus amounts for me and my group. The women in my group were even more upset about this than I was. By the time I could confront everyone concerning this, the woman vice president had been fired and the advertising manager had quit. He had seen the handwriting on the wall, for the new senior vice president who had fired and replaced the woman vice president seemed determined to replace everyone she had hired. Once the new senior vice president was in place, very few of the marketing managers who had reported to the woman were left.

Knowing that the new senior vice president was going to reorganize my group, I decided to gather all job descriptions (which I had developed for my group), projects, goals, and accomplishments and to ask to be allowed to continue to manage the group. I showed him the memos and documentation acknowledging me as manager of the group, for I was afraid that he might try to say that I had reported to the advertising manager and that he had been responsible for my group's accomplishments. I did not trust him and that is why I supported my presentation to him with the appropriate documentation. He promised to read everything and get back to me.

In his reorganization of the marketing effort, he reclaimed the industry marketing group and the attractive young Southern woman who had first been hired as my assistant. Then he announced that my group would be managed by this young woman. Here I go again. Someone whom I had trained and who knew nothing about my group was to be my manager. Of course, I refused to comply with this decision. When the senior vice president asked why, I simply said, ''I trained her and she is not capable of managing me.''

I really do not know what I expected him to do. I was prepared to quit, but I know he wanted to avoid repeating that scene with the Boss and the top executive. I also feel that he had been told by the Boss to let me do whatever I wanted to. So, he asked, ''What group do you want to be in?'' Again I was faced with naming the position I wanted. This must say something about either my competence or their fear that I would sue. I wondered why they did not just fire me. But they knew I was aware that they needed grounds for dismissal. I was really feeling uncomfortable with a company that had treated me most unfairly and without cause except racism and sexism, but I had decided to stick it out. I was hoping to force them to deal with me. I wanted them to specify why I was being passed over; I wanted them to be honest with me and with themselves. But they could not. They wanted to believe that others were better qualified, but they knew they were not. So they dealt with me by letting me choose my job.

I considered all of the new senior vice president's proposed groups. I also considered the managers who had been named. I had more seniority, marketing experience, and intelligence than all of them. They were all white and mostly male. Not one of the few women managers who had been identified was over forty or bigger than a size eight. (Somehow most women, white and black, think age and appearance are factors. Perhaps they are.) I chose the one group that did not as yet have a manager. It also had but one member, a white male. I thought that I could possibly have some input in managing it. The group was sales training. I was already providing the effective presentations portion of that training; and at that point, corporate sales training consisted of little else.

My group members were devastated when I told them who their new manager would be. They were shocked and hurt for me and knew that I would never report to the woman I had trained. They all knew that I would either quit or request a transfer to another group. Two of the group members also asked to be transferred to different groups. Some of their proposed new manager's past escapades had caused them to lose respect for her, and they could not accept her as their boss. The feeling of the group was that we had all thought that things could not get any worse than they had been under the woman vice president, but they had.

The new senior vice president questioned each group member privately and asked her to discuss her honest feelings about the changes in management. Whenever any one of them actually did express her feelings candidly and those feelings differed from those of the senior vice president, she suffered for it. From that point on she was not viewed as a team player; she was omitted from the infamous bonuses (I certainly was omitted from the following bonus period—the first and only bonus from which I was ever omitted); and she was not considered for any future management positions. Most of the members of that group eventually either left the company or transferred to different offices. The people were not the key; the senior vice president and his choices were.

When the attractive young Southern woman was asked why I had refused to report to her, she simply said, "Margie did not think that it was appropriate." She was right. It wasn't!

12

Becoming the Trainer

$\mathcal{T}$he sales training department began with two employees, a white male and me. Both of us had previously worked as presales system consultants and both of us felt qualified to manage the department. But the new senior vice president had his own ideas about the department's management. He told us that the department needed to be managed by someone who had previously been in direct sales—in other words, a salesman.

There is some validity to his taking this position, although most successful salesmen are not very good managers or trainers. In fact, most successful salesmen are interested neither in managing others nor in teaching them to sell. They are more interested in selling themselves. Be that as it may, the senior vice president called a meeting to announce his choice for manager of the sales training department.

His choice happened to be a person with whom I was very familiar. I had accompanied him on one of his first sales calls for the company. He was a novice, and even the Boss considered me the senior in charge of closing that sale. By the time he was appointed manager of the sales training department he had had one fairly successful year, but had not been overwhelmingly successful with the company. I viewed him as being both very young and immature. However, having learned through bitter past experience not to be completely honest with this senior vice president, when asked what I thought of my new manager, I simply replied, "He's trainable."

Knowing that my new manager knew nothing about education and training and very little about sales, I realized that I would be expected to organize the department, develop curriculums, and teach courses. While I was busy doing all of these things, my young, white male manager would make the important decisions and most of the money. In fact, he admitted to me that he had been paid quite a healthy sum of money to accept the position, nearly twice as much as I was making. I was very much disturbed by this realization and knew that I would not be happy with this arrangement. Had he been an intelligent manager, he never would have discussed his salary with one of his employees.

So I decided to take a wait and see attitude and do only what I was told. The other employee in our department used my lack of initiative to propose his own departmental plan. He soon became frustrated by the fact that his plans were presented to the senior vice president as the manager's own. I had expected as much, but since I had decided long ago that I was not playing the corporate game I did not let it bother me. I just continued to do the best possible job I could in teaching my effective presentations course and waited to see what training ideas my manager would offer.

My manager exhibited no management skills, no interpersonal skills, and had no training experience. He was aware that he lacked the requisite background for his position and enrolled in several courses to learn about sales training. He did not even attempt to manage me or the other departmental member, but he did hire a secretary whom he very ineffectively did try to manage. His feeble efforts only distressed her, and I found myself constantly directing her work. Even though I had decided to back away from departmental management, I could not resist helping one who was so completely confused and mismanaged.

About this time my doctor advised me that I would need major surgery. I saw this pending hospital stay and convalescence as an opportunity to get away from the company for a while and to consider my future employment options. Because of my tenure with the company, I was eligible for thirteen weeks of long-term disability with full compensation. I took twelve of them.

During that time I thought about my future with MSA and looked for another job. I discovered that I made more money than most other Atlanta companies were willing to pay a black woman, and the positions that I was considering were no better than the one I had. There was prejudice, racism, and sexism everywhere I looked, and the benefits and seniority I had established with MSA would be lost. So I decided to return to MSA and the sales training position, do the best job I could, and expect no rewards. This was easier said than done. There was something about the way I had been raised that made me want to excel and to expect rewards regardless of my race or sex. I still believed that I was better than most of my white male colleagues and that being better was rewarded.

Upon my return, my male departmental colleague had decided to resign. He had been told that he had no future with the company. He was given time off to look for another job. He was told that he could do better elsewhere, that he could find a place where he would have the opportunity to manage, and that his skills were not needed as I had all the educational skills and the manager had the selling background the department required. Although he was indirectly fired, he was given a going away party and wished well by all who knew him. This party was just another example of the hypocrisy that ran rampant throughout the company.

His leaving left me in the position of running the department, for the manager did not even pretend to know what to do. Even though I had told myself that I was not playing the corporate game and that I would do only what was absolutely required and requested of me, I found myself taking control. It was impossible for me not to. I had too much pride in my work and ability to let anything I was associated with fail. I determined the agendas, established a certification procedure for marketing representatives and system consultants, supervised the secretary, and continued to teach the classes that had been suspended during my convalescence. Incidentally, I was told that there was no one else qualified to teach my classes, so they had been suspended until my return. If I was to believe that I was too incompetent to manage the department, I wonder why no one else was qualified to teach my classes.

The manager attended the management meetings, proposed the material I had prepared for him, and continued to make the important decisions. He was quite content with my doing his work for him, and at this point I had tried to convince myself that I did not care. I kept reminding myself that I was working to save money to help my sons go to college, and I reasoned that any sacrifice I made that helped them was well worth it.

We added a new member to our team, a young woman who was a recent college graduate. Our manager literally gave her to me. He brought her into my office and told me to train her, give her work to do, and see that she learned everything about the department. I could see the attractive young Southern woman all over again and wondered whether this young woman would also grow up to be proposed as my manager. But this young woman was so eager to learn and so in awe of me that I pushed all negative thoughts from my mind and took her under my wing. I suppose my strong mothering instinct was surfacing again. She was a very bright student who proved to be completely loyal to me throughout her tenure with the department and is still a much valued friend.

I advised the manager to seek outside consultant help in teaching selling techniques to the sales representatives, and he began that search. He always responded quickly to my advice, for I did not offer it often and he trusted my judgment.

In the meantime, the company again began to undergo extensive reorganization. The microcomputer software company was sold, some jobs were eliminated, and some new positions with our parent company were created. The Southern Gentleman, being one of the "good old boys," was given one of these positions. I kept thinking that they had missed the perfect opportunity to rid themselves of him along with the microcomputer software company, but he had not yet risen to his level of incompetence and he was saved. The football player was also saved. I guess Georgia Tech graduates do look out for their own.

Top executives decided that the company should be reorganized to accommodate industry specialization. Industry subgroups were named and all marketing personnel were assigned to one of these groups. This subgrouping provided a new source of executive in-fighting, for each executive wanted responsibility for the industry in which future growth was anticipated.

My manager did find a consultant experienced in teaching industry selling strategies, and he convinced the company to hire this instructor in a consulting capacity. My task was to schedule every marketing person in the company to attend the training within a relatively short period of time. The Southern Gentleman, in his new marketing position, was to work with me on this assignment. I was amused when we began to work together. He was to provide me with a list of all of the system consultants in all of our offices along with their industry specialties. Then I was to arrange a schedule so that no office would be depleted of any industry specialty and all personnel would be trained as quickly as possible.

When I asked him for his list, he simply said, "Margie, no one knows the consultants better than you do. You really don't need my help." When there was work to be done, I was the authority on interoffice personnel; but when a promotion was in question, those I had trained, like the football player, knew more people and were known better than I was. Remember that this same Southern Gentleman failed to promote me because I was "not well known in the other offices." The blatant racism that I had suspected was confirmed by his statement. The original hurt and disappointment that I had experienced during the time I was being passed over resurfaced. But I had been given an assignment, and finding him to be of no help at all, I proceeded without him.

A short while later, the rest of the company found the Southern Gentleman to be as worthless as I had, and he quietly left the company. Eventually even being a white male Georgia Tech graduate could not save him from his own incompetence.

The scheduling job I had undertaken did not stop with the system consultants; it also included the marketing representatives. In order to obtain their names and areas of concentration, I had to confer with top executives. Again I was told, "Margie, everyone knows you and because of their respect for you, they will do whatever you tell them. Just arrange the schedule." So it appeared that I was highly respected, well known, well liked, but not promotable. Racism.

The scheduling did turn out to be a Herculean task, but I accomplished it, and everyone was trained. My manager, who was totally dependent on me, did appreciate my efforts and tried to have me rewarded. However, the vice president, now also a senior vice president, with whom I had previously had the shouting match had carefully placed one of his team members in the marketing department. As I view it, the primary purpose of this placement was to keep an eye on the new senior vice president who had replaced my mentor as the vice president's new competition for the next promotion. A much less important purpose for this placement was to make sure that I was never rewarded or recognized for anything. Remember that the Boss had reprimanded him for arguing with me and had told him to stay away from me, so he had decided to get even.

How did I know any of this? My manager, young and inexperienced, had no better sense than to tell me what happened behind closed doors in the marketing managers' meetings. I know that he was telling me the truth because I had several other friends in those meetings who confirmed what I was told.

When my manager suggested that I receive a reward for the tremendous amount of work I had done in the scheduling of all marketing personnel for training, the opposing team "plant" was reported to have said, "What was so difficult about that job? My secretary could have done it." Everyone knew that none of the marketing people would have cooperated with his secretary and that she did not know enough about them or their specific responsibilities to have accomplished the difficult scheduling task. But behind closed doors, it is not worth the effort to fight for someone against whom there is strong opposition. My manager did not bother to fight for me.

This same "plant" continued to ask, "What is so special about Marge Kimbrough? She is overpaid and really does not do anything." He added some extremely derogatory racial slurs that even my manager and my friends would not repeat. One such slur prompted a female manager to leave the room in disgust. The purpose of these remarks was to discredit me in such a way that my manager would be reluctant to ever propose my name again for any reward. It was well known that my manager had little backbone.

The derogatory comments about me so disturbed my manager that he asked what the plant had against me. When I explained the plant's relationship to the opposing vice president and my past encounters with that vice president, even my manager with all of his naïveté understood. My manager then tried to tell me that he was a top salesman and that he would sell my talents and abilities to his management so that I would receive the credit I deserved. The purpose of this comment was to keep me working hard for him. It is difficult to sell someone else when you are busy taking credit for that person's work. I knew full well what he was doing, but I pressed on—believing that I had no other options if I intended to stay with the company. I had faith that God would reward me, if not within the company, then in some other way. I felt like the three Hebrew boys in the fiery furnace: My God was able to deliver and reward me. Even if he did not, I knew that he was able.

Feeling spiritually renewed, I decided to pay a visit to the Boss and ask him about the comments that had so greatly disturbed me. I realized that I was bypassing the senior vice president, but in my opinion he was part of the problem. I wanted to know why there was the feeling that I was so incompetent. I also wanted the Boss to know what was happening in the senior vice president's management meetings.

The Boss immediately agreed to see me, and he was very friendly during the meeting. He acted as though he was genuinely surprised that I was being spoken of in such negative terms. He even commented that when he asked the senior vice president who would follow up in the offices with the training that had begun, my name had been proposed. He said that he (the Boss) had responded that I was perfect for that assignment. I was a proven instructor and well known and respected in all the offices.

I was interested to hear that the senior vice president would speak very highly of me in the presence of the Boss, whom he knew liked me, but would not open his mouth in my defense when the "plant" was degrading me. This is typical behavior of a gamesman. You agree with the flow of the conversation. You play politics with people's lives. If it is beneficial for you to agree—that is, if your superior is speaking—then you agree with whatever is being said. If the position being taken will not in any way benefit you, you remain silent. Integrity does not enter into your game plan.

I explained to the Boss that I had very little faith in the senior vice president and none at all in the competence of my manager, but he said that he had a lot of faith in the senior vice president and asked me to be patient with my manager. He reminded me that my manager was new at managing and I would have to *teach* him to be a good manager.

The Boss promised to work on my problem; he told me not to worry and said that he would "get back to me." The Boss discussed what I had said with the senior vice president, who in turn discussed it with my manager. My manager then called me into his office. He was very hurt because I had not come to him. I explained that there was nothing he could do. Then he wanted to know why I had not told him that I was going to talk to the Boss. He said that he knew that the Boss's office door was always open to me because of our past working relationship, but that he wished that I had told him that I was planning to enter that door.

I explained to him that I had not informed him of my plans because I knew that he would tell the senior vice president, thus giving him time to "get his lie together." I still believe that forewarned is forearmed. My manager even admitted that he would have told the senior vice president.

My manager continued the discussion by telling me that the senior vice president said to him, "You see how much your speaking up for her got you. She went to the Boss, reported you, and now I have been told that she has a management problem." That statement was certainly accurate, but I knew that it meant that nothing would be done about it. By telling the senior vice president that I had a management problem, the Boss meant for

him to fix it. The Boss believed that when he told someone to fix
something, it would be fixed. It wasn't.

I actually even went to the Boss one more time requesting a
transfer to a newly acquired division, but again, nothing ever
came of it. I am sure the Boss had more pressing concerns than
whether or not Marge Kimbrough was happy in her current job
assignment. Over the years I also had learned that the Boss
believed that if you ignored a problem long enough, it would go
away. Eventually that philosophy proved to be true.

Additional staff and functional areas of responsibility were
added to the position of manager of sales training. He continued
to make decisions but failed to assume any of the day-to-day
responsibilities. If people needed managing and I did not do it,
they went unmanaged. I could not refuse to help those who
asked me for direction, but I refused to assume complete
control. After all, I was not being paid to manage and I would
not be rewarded for managing. I simply did the best job I could
personally be satisfied with, and this, though not the best I could
have done, was better than anything my manager could have
done. He was elated.

My manager would often arrive to find most of the staff in my
office receiving instructions and guidance for pending classes
and daily responsibilities. He would stop at my office, ask what
was going on, and then instruct me to carry on. As long as I was
willing to lead, he was willing to let me. He would often call me
into his office and ask why everyone always came to me for
direction. I tried to explain a little about maturity and
interpersonal and management skills, but my words fell on deaf
ears.

After I had successfully developed and conducted the
evaluation and certification of new North American marketing
personnel, my manager decided to conduct the same evaluation
and certification in Europe. Because he knew that he did not
have the technical expertise to conduct the process alone, he

invited a white male technician to accompany him. The only problem was that neither of them knew anything about my certification procedures. Of course, I was not invited to go. After all, he had never been to Europe, and he certainly did not want to be traveling in the company of a black woman.

So he did the next best thing. He asked me to provide him with daily agendas detailing what was to be done during each hour. I was to place in separate folders the test (with answers), the schedules, the rooms, and the necessary equipment and personnel, in other words, everything so that he would know exactly what to do. I handed him everything he needed. I was sure that he would not even have to think. But just before he was to leave, he came into my office with a microcassette tape recorder that he shoved in my face and said, ''Now say exactly what I should say each day before I conduct the certification.''

I was shocked, but not too shocked to respond to him, ''I am not your mother, and you will not take my voice with you. I have more than sufficiently provided you with what you will need. If you cannot handle it from here, stay at home!'' He was too inept to understand my reaction, but he was so afraid of antagonizing me and losing his free ride that he brought me and the other members of our department who were loyal to me gifts back from Europe.

The next time he got ready to go to Europe for certification, he asked for the same folders of information, but he did not shove the tape recorder in my face. This time, in addition to a technician, he took his wife. She had never been to Europe either, and when one is in a management position there ought to be, according to his thinking, some benefits. There were still departmental gifts upon his return, but the gifts were much less expensive. I am sure that his wife told him that he was being much too generous. She did not know that he was totally dependent on me. Wives never do, for they have complete faith in their husbands' abilities.

Feeling successful with having brought in an outside consultant to teach selling strategies and having organized through me curriculums and certification procedures, my manager decided to take examples of everything with him and seek employment elsewhere. He was looking for a vice presidential title and stock in a new company so that he would have something to leave his children. After all, he was a white male, and for him the sky was the limit. His level of confidence was high even if his level of competence was low.

In his search for a new position he used me as a reference. I told him that I would be honest about his temper tantrums and immature behavior, but he still sold himself to a new company and got his vice presidential position. When he told me about it, I responded by reminding him to look at our company. It was easy to see that vice presidential titles were a dime a dozen. He laughed.

He told me that he was not sure who would replace him, and although he knew that I had done most of his work, he was quite sure that I would not be named manager of the group. He admitted that racism ran rampant through the company. This of course was extremely discouraging to hear voiced so openly, and yet it was not surprising.

When I discussed the situation with the senior vice president, he admitted that everyone knew that I was the educational and training guru and that my manager was "just a salesman," but that he thought that it was important to have a salesman as the manager. Again I was told that I would have to help train another manager. When I asked what was in it for me, I was told that I was paid a good salary and I received bonuses when no one else in my group did. I know that I should have been happy since I had decided that I was not playing the game, but I was not. I felt that I was being used.

It is hard to go to work every day and perform at your best level only to be told that you will never be considered for promotion. Even when you decide that you are not playing the corporate game, you still expect to be rewarded, praised, or in some way recognized. I was told to be thankful that I had a job. I suppose the reference was to the white male who had "resigned" from our department because he had been told that he had no real future there. I was needed to train others to manage, but in truth I had no future there either. I am sure that they were all afraid of how I might react if they admitted it to me.

A new woman vice president had been named, and my manager reported to the senior vice president through her. She asked me to continue to provide leadership to the group until a new manager could be selected. I did not begin to do anything that I had not already been doing, and some of the most successful training courses our department had conducted were conducted after our so-called manager had left.

By the beginning of 1987 a new sales training manager had been named. Again he was a white male with previous direct sales experience. Like his predecessor, he had had some success in sales but had finished 1986 near the bottom of the sales list. It still seemed to be true that those who finished near the top of the sales list were interested not in managing, but in selling.

Also like his predecessor, he knew nothing of education and training and asked me to continue to provide leadership to the group. By this time the group had been reduced to the manager, myself as a training specialist, and a training coordinator/secretary. All other group members had been fired or shifted to other positions in the company. The new manager had plans to eventually take over all training in the company and to greatly expand the certification program I had begun.

It was this latter plan that led to my decision to leave. The manager asked me to explain the certification process that I had developed. I did that. Then he asked if everything I had told him

was documented. I responded, "Of course." Then he asked to
see a copy of the documentation and asked me to submit a list of
ways to improve the process. He said that he intended to give all
of my documentation and suggestions for improvements to
someone that he would hire from one of the field offices as
manager of certification. When I asked him what I would do
when this new manager took over, he said that I could develop
course curriculums and assist the manager of certification.

As I saw it, I had already developed a process that I now had
the opportunity to improve. However, I was asked to hand
everything over to my new field boss, who would get the credit
for all of my work. I would at that point not only again be
training and doing all the work for the manager of certification,
but also for his manager (the new sales training manager). With
this in mind, I decided that it was just not worth the effort
anymore. I had been used and abused long enough, and I started
writing my letter of resignation.

13

Deciding on a New Life

❧

*T*he decision to resign was also a decision to lead a new life, one away from corporate America. Although I had previously thought about resigning, I had never really considered not looking for another job in the data processing industry. By this time I knew that corporate America had nothing further to offer me, and I had already given it all of the time and energy I intended to. I often wondered why I had already given it so much.

My husband was extremely supportive of my decision, for he knew that I was not willing to stand idly by while still another less competent person, whom I had already trained or would have to train, was made my manager. It still amazes me that management thought that I would forever be content to train less competent white males and to allow them to consider themselves my manager. As the old folks say, "Even iron wears out," and my patience had worn out. I had had it!

I carefully worded my letter of resignation to reflect my sentiments, and it read as follows:

> During my fourteen years with MSA, I have observed individuals with inferior talent, educational background, company knowledge, and professional experience progress

while I have retrogressed. Therefore, I can only conclude that
my assessment of my abilities differs from management's
assessment of my abilities.

Although I have consistently performed exceptionally well
and have had glowing reports submitted about my work with the
field and with various corporate departments, I have received
meager bonuses and raises. While, on the other hand, the
generous bonuses and raises have been reserved for the
managers whom I have trained and most of whose work I have
consistently done.

Fourteen years is a long time to invest in one organization;
and, if one's contribution is neither appreciated nor rewarded, it
is too long. Therefore, I submit my resignation effective April
10, 1987.

I addressed my resignation to my manager and copied his
manager who was the woman vice president, her manager who
was the senior vice president, the Boss, and the top executive.

My manager, being new in his position and not very familiar
with me, was shocked. After reading my letter, he said that he
understood how I felt but had no idea what I had been through.
His statement was a reflection of his ignorance and incompetence. As a new manager, he should have taken it upon himself
to find out all he could about the backgrounds, work
experience, and talents of each of his departmental members.
This would have been especially easy, for at the time he was
made manager, the department consisted of me and the
secretary.

The senior vice president made an appointment to see me. He
came to my office, asked what this resignation business was all
about, and judging by the smile on his face, seemed somewhat
relieved with the prospect of not having to deal with me
anymore. He said that he understood what courage it took to
quit and that he believed that if one is miserable and dreads
going to work, one should resign. I let him know in no uncertain

terms that I was not miserable and did not dread going to work. I told him that I did not depend on my job for happiness, for I had an inner joy that neither he nor the job had given to me and certainly neither could take that joy away. I was resigning because I was tired of encountering atrocious prejudice and abuse. I was unwilling to continue to train his managers for him; I would no longer be his educational guru.

When he asked what I was going to do, I told him that I would do some consulting, some public speaking, and even if I did nothing, my husband was well able to support me. Somehow my last comment seemed to disturb him. I felt that he was wondering what black preacher made enough money to sustain the loss of substantial income like mine. He did not know that while my career was retrogressing under his management, my husband's career had progressed to the point of being the pastor of the largest United Methodist church in the southeastern United States. It also has the distinction of being the largest predominantly black United Methodist church in the world.

My perception that white men do not feel that black men make enough money to support non-working wives was reenforced by one of the marketing vice presidents, the one whom I have previously identified as the "plant." When I was asked by another employee what I would be doing when I stopped working, he responded, "Starving to death." My natural inclination was to tell this vice president, for whom there was certainly no love lost, that his wife did not work and they were not starving. Surely my husband was at least as good if not a better provider than he was. But I just chalked it up to racism and ignored him. His comments did not stop there, for during my going-away party, he stopped by to remark, "What's all this? I thought we waited to have the party after they left." Even in my leaving he was still trying to discredit me, and I am sure that it was all the work of the vice president, the one with whom I had previously had the shouting match. For some reason they just could not let me go in peace. They wanted to try to break my spirit, but it did not work because I had talked it over with the Lord, and we were of one accord.

The woman vice president invited me to lunch. She confessed that she had wondered how I had survived so long. She knew that I had been discriminated against, but she was playing the corporate game and it was all she could do to survive herself. I thought of the other woman vice president who had decided to play the game, and I wondered if her fate would be the same. I was sure that it would, for not only was there the blatant racism that I had faced, but there was also sexism, which we both faced.

She told me that the Boss often commented that I was one of the most intelligent employees in the company, but he felt that my family came first. I suppose she said this to justify my not having advanced further with the company. I told her that if in fact I was an intelligent and valued employee, I certainly should have been rewarded. I went on to say that not many years ago I was making twice as much money as my husband, but he had passed me. She responded, "Your husband has a career, but you have a job." People need jobs to support themselves and their families; I did not need a job.

Realizing that the conversation regarding my lack of a career was getting us nowhere, I directed the conversation to her career. I advised her to join the vice president's team, and I relayed some of my experiences with him and his "plant." I told her that if she was not on his team helping him, he would probably seek to destroy her. I think she listened and heeded my advice, for shortly after I left she became a part of his organization. Although many people thought that she had invited me to lunch to try to convince me to stay, most of the time was spent with me giving her advice. She knew that she had nothing to offer me, for she, although a vice president, had no power. No woman in the company did.

I never heard from the Boss at all. I am sure that he was more than a little hurt because I had not discussed my intention to resign with him before I submitted my letter, but I was tired of talk. Each time I had talked with him before, nothing had happened. I had decided that he was not interested in helping to solve my problem; he was just waiting for me to accept things the way they were. I could not.

The top executive did call me, and he told me that he actually had made an effort to find me a position within the company in which I would feel fulfilled. But there was none. He also told me that if he had been given more time, he could have worked something out. But he could not have, for there was nothing to work out. The "good old boy" promotion policy was well entrenched in the organization. He did express a feeling of remorse because I had not talked with him during any of the previous instances in which I had felt that I was experiencing discrimination. But I explained that I had talked with the Boss and nothing had been done. He responded, "You talked with the wrong person." He pretended not to know that for me there was no right person.

I do not think anything or anyone could have gotten me to change my mind. I knew that I had to leave and that I needed to write down what had happened. I had had so many experiences as a black woman in corporate America. I had been the first and the only in so many instances, yet I was convinced that I was not alone in what I had experienced. I also felt that there would be many other young black women graduating from college at the top of their classes expecting to progress up the corporate ladder. I knew they needed to hear my story and perhaps benefit from my experiences. If just one is better able to prepare herself for the road ahead, my journey will have had meaning.

I can recall several incidents in which intelligent, ambitious young black men and women were hired by MSA. They came to talk with me wondering why I was not a vice president. They knew that I had certainly been with the company long enough and they had been exposed to some of my contributions to past company success. They were also well aware that many of those who were vice presidents were not nearly as well qualified. I told them that there were many excuses but racism was probably high on the list. Their response was always the same, "If they did not promote you, they surely will not promote me. You are much better qualified than I am." Most of them left the company before I did.

Shortly after I resigned, a young black woman who worked for the Georgia Power Company shot two of her supervisors and killed herself because she had been passed over for a promotion.[1] It appeared that the young woman had already been doing the new job for several weeks and would be expected to train the white man who actually got the promotion. In her suicide note she said that the type of unfairness that she had experienced was happening everywhere and it had to be stopped. She felt that her actions would give other supervisors something to think about when they were contemplating unfair promotions.

After this incident appeared in the paper, many of my friends called and said that they had thought of me. I told them that I would not have considered harming anyone and certainly not myself. First of all it would have been against my Christian relationship with God, and, second, no one who had ever passed me over for promotion was worth my dying for, or in fact, worth my killing. I had too much to live for, and the job was not my whole life. No job should be.

---

1. Fran Hesser and Wanda Yancey, "Suicide Note Alleges Racial Bias," *The Atlanta Journal* and *The Atlanta Constitution* (Saturday, April 25, 1987), pp. 1A and 22A.

I have encountered atrocities, and others are still encountering them. But after twenty-eight years of dealing with those atrocities, I have decided to begin a new life. I know that there are books to write, classes to teach, speeches to make, meals to cook, family and friends to love, "and miles to go before I sleep."[2]

2. Robert Frost, "Stopping by the Woods on a Snowy Evening," *A Little Treasury of Modern Poetry* (New York: Charles Scribner's Sons, 1952), p. 132.

EPILOGUE

What have I learned from it all? I have learned that a black woman's corporate success is dependent upon her beginning. She must be raised with an air of superiority and an attitude of confidence. She must know that she is not just better than some, but better than most. She must know that she can compete and that she is a winner.

She must be willing to work long and hard, unquestionably committed to her corporate success. She must have the educational and experiential credentials to support her efforts toward measurable accomplishments. She must be willing to sacrifice her family, friends, even religious affiliations, and all personal interests whenever and however the job demands.

She must be an ardent student of the corporate game, learning to play it well. She must be chosen by a sponsor and may even be tempted to soften her moral standards. She must keep her eyes and ears open at all times and take advantage of any opportunities that are presented.

She must be attractive, trim, well-groomed, looking the part of the corporate executive. She must wear simple, expensive, well-tailored clothes. She must never forget that she is a black woman and that white men desire her.

She can be successful in white corporate America. I suppose

that one of the real atrocities I encountered was the discovery
that I was not she. Yes, this discovery was an atrocity because I
would have been a wonderful executive, and I could have
contributed immensely to the success of any company. It was
also an atrocity to discover that the woman I have described is
the only type of black woman who has a possibility of being
successful in corporate America where racism is still alive and
well. I do not regret not being that woman, for I am happy with
the woman that I am. Mama was right; I am better, and I thank
God that I am!